Their Own Bare Hands

poems from the
Bridgewater International Poetry Festival 2015

Sarah Evans, editor

UNBOUND
CONTENT

Englewood, NJ

ISBN 978-1-936373-57-4
Published in the United States by Unbound Content, LLC, Englewood, NJ.
Cover art: © 2017 Kate Hanna
The poems in this collection are all original and previously unpublished with the exception of those listed in the credits page at the end of the volume.

THEIR OWN BARE HANDS
First edition 2017

in the middle of the square
there were long diaphanous hands
hands thick and veined as chipolatas
gnarled hands that cried for solace
craftman's hands mottled with splinters
hands whose fingers knew the printed word
so intimately, the whorls could be read in italics
and whilst all hands are pure and innocent
some of them, lovingly manicured
belonged to high class thieves
others, downy as a foal's nape
glinted with particles of cocaine dust

from Albert Russo's "Dissolving the Masquerade"

Contents

Introduction

This anthology is the culmination of the second Bridgewater International Poetry Festival. On a chilly January weekend, more than 70 poets brought with them a taste of the world through their eyes and the richness of their diverse experiences in the form of poetry.

Though the general "theme" of the 2015 anthology is centered on the global community of poets, and the ways that poems connect us, many other motifs arose as I heard and then compiled these poems. I was an eager front-row observer in one room of the festival for several days straight, taking in the images, feelings, thoughts, and memories.

Love, loss, heritage, war, poverty, family connections (or dysfunction), life struggles, aging, overcoming demons and traumas of the past, even meditations on poetry itself, can be found within these pages. The result has been a moving collection of distinct perspectives that blend to comment on humanity and the human condition.

Albert Russo's "Dissolving the Masquerade" provided the inspiration for the title of this collection. Hands are a particularly significant subject of my own art and poetry, and in Russo's rendition, hands not only reveal the lives they empower, as seen in the excerpt in previous pages, but also become the sole representatives of their owners–the connection that the people have to the world. In a single moment, "in the middle of the square/the people had all but vanished/leaving in their stead/the only possession they had/THEIR OWN BARE HANDS."

I found this concept to be a meaningful expression of the poems that I heard, and of the poets who wrote them. I hope you enjoy this anthology that you hold in your own hands—your hands are included in this community, too.

Sarah Evans, Editor

Dissolving the Masquerade

Albert Russo

for some mysterious reason,
in the middle of the pedestrian square,
they felt their clothes loosen and fray
like dandelions caught by a storm
and, averting each other's eyes
as that mute and invisible alien
stripped them to the skin,
they suddenly stopped running about

    in the middle of the square
    never had there been such a sight
    hands twirling like mad dervishes
    hands that spun more swiftly
    than the windmills of Friesland
    hands which played legerdemain
    for an unpaying and bedazzled audience

in the middle of the square
the people had all but vanished
leaving in their stead
the only possession they had
THEIR OWN BARE HANDS

in the middle of the square
there were long diaphanous hands
hands thick and veined as chipolatas
gnarled hands that cried for solace
craftman's hands mottled with splinters
hands whose fingers knew the printed word
so intimately, the whorls could be read in italics
and whilst all hands are pure and innocent
some of them, lovingly manicured
belonged to high class thieves
others, downy as a foal's nape
glinted with particles of cocaine dust
the birds that nested under the awnings of the square
feasted their eyes upon this choreography in Hands Major

twittering to their hearts' delight
as surely they must have eons ago
long, long before their biped cousins
had invented the art of masquerade

in the middle of the square
through the whims of gods
for a fraction of eternity
man had only nature
to clothe his soul

One Line to Live

Patsy Asuncion

Life is not a straight line,
nor a tidy row of dashes.
It's more a series of periods
with question marks and slashes.

Sometimes a comma gives
us pause to glimpse our substance
as we ponder obscure asterisks
in search of God's existence.

There must be more to life
than colons and their lists,
some secrets in parentheses
to reveal the way to bliss.

It's easier to exist by
another's quotation marks,
hide ourselves in backspaces
than write our own remarks.

I choose to live my life,
one line per situation,
risk grammatical errors,
trust my own punctuation.

Everything Makes Music When It Burns

R.G. Evans

Everything makes music when it burns—
destruction is the rougher side of art
where char and embers harmonize in turns.

Until you live your life within these terms
your sadness may conceal the beauty part:
that everything makes music when it burns.

The aria within our body churns
with smoke and blackened ruins of our hearts
where char and embers harmonize in turns.

We're fuel, and when we carbonize it forms
etudes and scales, and passion's complex charts.
Everything makes music when it burns.

A skilled musician finds he can discern
a symphony where conflagrations start,
where char and embers harmonize in turns,

and even when it's all collapsed and worms
make homes inside the burned out vital parts,
still everything makes music when it burns.
The char and embers harmonize in turns.

Originally published in Tiferet.

Aliens and Companions
Sirwan Kajjo

Compose a poem from your cracked lips!
With a strange pen, write the story of your life
slowly.
Repeat your childhood games.
Retrieve the scent of sun
from between your fingers.
Make summer nights as joyful as
they were before!
Merge cry with laughter,
as you used to do every year.

Revive your success symphony
one more time and
brighten my nerves.

Drink your morning coffee
at the window without being shy
and
let its smoke fill in my nose…
Go to the market again and
Bring a bagful of fruits and vegetables with you

Lock the door of the shop and
come back home swiftly,
before the sharp sun damages
the receding hairline of your head.

Why I Disagree with Bruegel and W.H. Auden
Beth Konkoski

As for suffering,
the old masters and poets may need some revision,
for they ignore those who wait,
who sit and wonder about a journey's completion.

The old masters and poets may need some revision.
Where is the thought for Icarus' mother?
Left to sit and wonder about a journey's completion
not made privy to her son's splash.

Where is the thought for Icarus' mother?
What would a mother say of waxed wings and the sun?
"No one suffers unregarded."
even if she never knows of her son's splash.

What would a mother say of waxed wings and the sun
should anyone ever bother to ask-
even if she never knows of her son's splash?
"We answer the terrifying phone in the empty pocket of night."

Should anyone ever bother to ask
the ring sears nightmares, slaughters sleep
that terrifying phone we answer in the empty pocket of night,
uncradling peace with the words we have longest feared.

Such a ring searing nightmares, slaughtering sleep,
ends hope and dreams and love,
uncradling peace with the words we have longest feared.
We inhale grief as it becomes ours.

Ignoring hope and dreams and love
you old masters must need some revision,
must acknowledge the grief as it becomes ours,
for somebody always notices the splash.

Shorn/I Almost Cut My Hair Today

Sarah Elizabeth Murphy

If it were to
grow
unending
it would be
all of me
less red,
less glistening,
woven
through
with the reality
of ever encroaching
grey.

It would trail
upon the floor,
caught in fingers
and doorways,
some days
wrapped
tight
and
pinned
upon my head.

Instead,
it is cut,
brushed,
teased
from root to tip.
Roughly
pulled
from passenger sides
to the gravel
of the ground.

Completely
twisted,
bound,
bleached
wrapped around itself
too many times;
banded
and
bonded
together.

Split ends
wandering away
from one another,
melanin slipping,
unbidden,
crimson,
to copper
to grey,
grey,
grey.

///

Let loose,
for the birds
to make nests of.

There Is

Joanna Lee

poetry. in the exquisite onslaught
of early May traintracks,
late night rainstorms, swooning

plumes of cavalry. a little
girl tips back a big bottle;
we compare commit-

ments, strawberries. i was
committed, once. it was
raining then, too. barefoot.

no white horses. no
pink rose. like the bath scents
i brought mother that

last time: rose, pink, bottle.
she never used them. this poem
is supposed to be

about other things, not
mothers&bottles: thunder,
the whistle of trains

in darkness. skipping
over rocks. barefoot
rivers can be

dangerous: no
white horses there,
either. it is

early May after all: who
will catch you? strawberry-
blonde, he called her.

she wrote him lovepoems
but even they were not
happy. fuck happy poems,

she tells me. poetry
is always barefoot. even
over broken glass.

An earlier version of "There is" was published in *Contemporary American Voices* (2012).

The Nobility of Poetry

Sara Robinson

Red blood flows
to a sea
but slowly
our hands
touch it and
it won't wash off

the nobility of poetry
lies in its ability
to state great truths
in a very very small space

to create an intimacy
with no pretense of
width or depth
height or time

an awareness
of the space itself
is to grant leave
for reverence of
this space with
its own dimension

the syllables
and strokes applied
will tell us everything
we need to know

O, the mastery of verse
clothed in satin phrases
it slips out from creases
   like an asp in hiding
to find its mark

First appeared in *Stones for Words* (Cedar Creek Publishing, 2014).

Pour Invoquer Le Poème

Sara Robinson

When you touch the pages
where I've written my words
do you feel a difference
are there rises and falls
or crests and valleys
perhaps a peak or plateau

Can my words caress your
fingers as they mark
your progress within
the strokes and turns

If you put a page next
to your cheek
do the fine hairs
there vibrate in waves
coming out to reach you

When you speak of poems
or engage them in your
conference perhaps you feel
a tingle of recognition
of some sense that means
these words may reach
inside you and rest at
last in that place you
reserve for special spirits

First appeared in *Stones for Words* (Cedar Creek Publishing, 2014).

Offering to My Fellow Poets

Albert Russo

a scathing review
should not cast you in a trance
though your blood cries out

are you stuck with words?
then string them around your neck
they will set you free

whatever they say
remember Kipling's advice
about self-control

a drop of honey
a taste of eternity
wrapped in syllables

thanks to the haiku
you can recreate the world
or leave not a trace

before man could speak
he knew poetry
by intuition

diplomacy
is the language one uses
when love has no place

like ships in the night
like clouds shredding in the blue
like your closing heart

the boat is sinking
but who thinks of the havoc
wrought in the ocean

travel to the stars
with your bag of memories
and earth's illusions

in desperation
let dreams carry you away
they'll color your pain

Creative Moods
Albert Russo

the act of writing
is like a plunge in the void
or a muffled sigh

when you're inspired
it is smooth as a pebble
swept by clear water

a storm breaks out
in the middle of the sentence
and the world is ablur

the room reeks of death
the stench is unbearable
dried rust-colored ink

it's been so long since
my fingers held a pen
they act arthritic

screen and computer
have replaced dad's Underwood
I hear his heartbeats

too much idleness
numbs the imagination
wind of a glacier

My small funeral

Sara Allam

In my small funeral
All my lovers will stand around
Holding poems they know were about them
Only killers know
A crime leaves a mark that doesn't wash away with death
A killer takes my book with his right hand
Pours ink on my picture
My staring picture like a carved drawing
Is now obscured by ink
But memory cannot hide it
The chair in the coffeehouse chatters
Tells his friends every day
About a serial killer
And a dress torn by an angry nail
Who saw on the killer's back the fingers of a fresh victim
There is no such thing as a perfect poem
Nor a perfect crime
Only one killer has all the pictures perfect in his eyes

Translated by Emad el Ahmad

A Fashion Model
Sara Allam

There is always an unwritten poem
Anguish caught in chest
I do not dare to commit
Cells that have died in the heart
Nerves stripped naked in the memory
Pictures growing paler to the eye
And voices I quiver upon hearing
A former fiancé whispers in his new wife's ear
The same words
The same details
As if he's giving her my favorite flower
From the only flower shop I love
My first love
Crosses a crowded street with his betrothed
I am a small picture in the background that no one sees
An old friend carrying my child on her chest
With a name I chose in his father's arms
Life is a skilled fashion model
Quickly changes her clothes
But always forgets the shoes

Verum and Factum *(After Giambattista Vico)*
Michael Trocchia

What to be made
of sparrows stuck

in the throat? What
to be made of the girl

gasping in the shed,
of dead trees holding up

sheaves of white sky,
of the hillside green

clean of human breath?

"Verum and Factum" first appeared in the *Worcester Review.*

Poem for the Back Cover of a Book
Jeff Schwaner

This book does not care if you buy it.
This poem does not care if you buy the book.
Even I do not care if you buy the book.
The three of us have been waiting here
to tell you this, but even more—perhaps
you have just been thinking of that person
whose love has kept you alive without you
knowing it these many years, perhaps you
are remembering that person now.
Are they right beside you, unaware your
love flows stronger than ever? Have you
not exchanged words in years? We are here
to tell you—put down this book, do not look
back, you were never looking back but always
straight through the eye of his soul.
Put down this book now and go to him.
Or, if you are still here, at a loss for words,
I will help you. Go buy this book
and leave it face down where he
will find it, and notice this poem,
that is why we are here, after all,
and we will see what can be done.

Poem Without Itself

Michael Trocchia

You lift one side
of the poem. Each

word slides
                    off
the page.
            Only punctuation
remains,
leaving this

  ordered silence—

a sheet of nothing
riddled
with periods

of loss.

On Translating Poetry from the Chinese
Jeff Schwaner

First you find a quiet place in the forest near a mountain. You set about clearing a small patch of land, building a house, moving a family in from the other side of the world, naturally they are confused at first, until you show them that everything is where it should be, including the dragon behind the falling water and beneath the icy pool and the distant dragon in the mountain and the fox behind the tombstone they cannot read and the toad on the moon and the orioles in the tree, and you set about showing them you have built the house where a breeze from the south protects against the red dust of the paths which led them here, and then you set about taking in the family's exiles, who naturally drink more wine than anyone else yet seem not to have the same sense of vertigo upon arrival, because the moon is the same and has always been the same moon and one day when you are out looking for one of them who did not come home last night you find a plant growing on the dusty path and take it home, and when you get there the exiles are waiting wondering where you were and if there is any more wine, and then you set about placing the perfect plant in a window on the top floor that the family loves and the forest around it loves and that sounds as the last needle of sun skims the canopy of trees and glances off the window like the sound of rain on bamboo. And in the leaves of that plant the past of each of the house's denizens has to be taken into account, and in every flower a future extending a thousand years. And then you turn your back on it as you turn your back on a dream upon waking, it has to melt back into the earth, artificial as it is, without causing harm. And the fox comes around looking for the garbage and in the middle of a clearing is the poem.

A Pen is a Pen is a Pen

Justin Walmsley

i met Gertrude Stein
on the tip, tipping forward on the tip of a pen
a pen belonging, having belonged, once, to elsewhere
this pen is homeless, now
tipping forward with Gertrude and myself
belonging to elsewhere, housed elsewhere
around this single pen, a tipping pen and poets poet'ting
tipping ink
tripping over pens tipping forward
a thousand Gertrude
belonging to blots of tipped over, into
ink, ink on a table, tables carved
allowing carvings suffused with ink
to dry a thousand Gertrude
no more ink
    than pen
        than blots of Gertrude tipping forward
           tripping myself otherwise, a homeless poet
               belonging to an otherwise homeless pen, myself
                  a homeless pen belonging to an elsewhere
                     elsewhere forward and otherwise gone.

lust poem no. 3

Joanna Lee

the spray over the rocks is
luminous; ducks
chase each other in
dark shallows; herons
fish in pairs, build nests
in high branches. you,

you make me want
new lingerie. i love the way
it looks like *linger*, like
that trick you did with the
strawberries, that time
we got tequila-drunk

at two in the afternoon. this
is the poem i should have
written then, weaving line
breaks into the space
between our breaths as we
dreamed of sea air.

but we are far
from the ocean here, do
our best with river-sand
and stolen seconds,
making silent promises
in sunlight that

the river carries to her mouth
& in her bones: *this will not
end as it should.*

An earlier version of "lust poem no.3" was published in *Contemporary American Voices* (2012).

lust poem no 4.
Joanna Lee

in his bed i am not afraid
of small crickets, fickle
engines or failure; find

the distance between here
and the ocean diminished, the
scent of our yesterday a river

dripping straight through
his thin striped sheets. he
licks expensive bourbon

from my bellybutton, says
the muscle in my back is
solid as frozen cod: i say

his irises could melt
icebergs & to swim with long
strokes in such waters i

would hop a boxcar and head
North with nothing. hungry, we
tear with our canines at cheek-

bones and pretenses below cover-
slipped copies of my old poems, re-
know what love there is in

ravish; for his tackle &
lure i would learn again
to fight, to drown.

Fire
Heather Banks

A match is struck,
kindling catches—
fire!
Limbs and branches transform again
to energy, to heat, to light.
Inside the fire, hands of flame
signal passionately,
tongues lick at darkness,
carry all away to nothingness
in the moment's heat.
The time of fire
is instant and forever.
Backlog of all experience
burns into the night
times and places known
and beyond memory—
sentinel against the dark of forgetting.
Heated atmosphere fades to dark
until we see no longer
ourselves, each other.
Our time, our meeting
exists only in the carbon date of ashes.

"Fire" is in her first chapbook, *Still Life Without Pomegranate* (2008).

Intimacy
Patsy Asuncion

I am your release
    as blush of bodies brushes
your music   as we pas de deux
boundless seas   your heart
    in a lifetime beat   as one
your lips   as we taste delicacies
uniquely ours   your grin as we feast
future memories

I am your hands
to bathe your weary body
    as you lose   your reach
your eyes   to hunt unseen
dangers   coming   your voice
    to your whispered hope
your ears   to sift through chatter
            to interpret the silence

I am your sky
    blue as cloudless hope
dissuading fears of unknown dawns
    your shoulders   to buttress slack
sails wearied by storm   your feet
to cushion the way through   arduous
disease   pausing in lavender
    to patter in beauty of moments.

Something About the Way She Touches

Michael Bassett

I'm watching the way she coaxes
him into hitting her again.
It is an intimate thing, weirdly
ritualistic, like my mother burying
a burnt turkey in the snow.
Something about the way she touches
the tip of her tongue to her bloody lip—
about the way his hand, red and hovering
somewhere between striking and reaching out—
reminds me of being a boy
in the backyard at twilight, waiting
for the wind to make something beautiful
from the tears of pear trees.

Us and Them
Michael Bassett

Her hair on my pillow is the peace I'd get as a kid coming in from the
ocean to the snoring air conditioning and the smells of coconut and
perch cooking. I want to write a poem for the tenderness I feel for
her knee socks, but instead I dream a solitary kestrel turns into a pale
winter sun and finally into my father's face bearded in foam and steam.
No matter how I keep his head submerged under my beet-colored
resentment, I'll always be in his study full of books too difficult for me.
The past should be more pliant. I hope here in this bed she and I are
parent-less, not caring about the legacies that crawl like Escher lizards
along a Möbius. But she may be lost in pills fetched for her mother. She
may be dreaming of her daddy's flannel shirts and her opening bedroom
door, the wand of light that doesn't reach.

Sings
Jesse Glass

She has come back from the dim cells
underground—my bride
still laved in dark honey
has cast off the paper coils
of the shadowless & taken
my shadow across her thin
blue shoulders.

Her hands move with a new mind
as light swells from between
the shards of the mirror
broken in madness. Her hands
pat the silver blades in place
& fly to daub her generous smile
with madder. She's returned

with Philippics & bon mots
dry eyed from the place where all must
weep & stands like a Daughter of Man
before my nakedness appraising
the amber lights burning in my flesh.

She has come back with ash
daubed on her neck & thighs
& with the stink of those fires
upon her. & in her hand she holds
an empty spool & makes the gesture
of wrapping one fine thread
Around it. Her wounds spiral open

without pain, their petals
the color of a tawdry ribbon. We
give stories to each one
and when she cries I laugh,
and when I cry, she opens
her torn mouth
& bravely sings.

define: *these windows*
Daniel Dissinger

because I saw you there
captured off-centered

like a breath of air
between your lips

slips
down

onto your throat

he watches for how
his body diminishes
into her neon city

...

it's better this way
it's how we'll remember
sleep and hunger

like fireplaces are supposed to fill a single room
with spark and not smoke

...

he stands at the edge
of some harrowing winter

like to cut some wrist open
is more beautiful
than undressing each other
in the dark
with our teeth

...

tell me that story you tell your children
where all these ghosts plant gardens
on the rooftops together

gardens where basil and cilantro run rampant
from east to west and it reminds us to cry
later gripped to each other like recorded phenomena

like divided here
like homeless

...

behind those curtains
she undresses his mouth
with olive oil

a closer simple grasp of lips
drench her breasts

what does it mean
to let go
of your ankles
in the middle
of the night

when all we ever desired
from each other
was tied tightly
around the bedposts

...

we somehow always lose the point

like when he says

it's complicated

when all she asked of him was

gently slice kiwis in the morning

that's what bodies crave before the sunrise

spills across dented parked cars

like how we would imagine new light

collapsed over bedrock in a shallow country creek

this is what freedom might taste like

someone's been lying here

waiting to be lifted out naked and dried

TOGETHER
A. Logan Hill

something that left me
walking in crusted snow
taking a long hot shower
music as if the speakers are in me
dreaming of a life called home
lived together in a matrimony
no one wanting
anything
from anyone else
living together like that
in the reminiscence
of a dream
some memory
staleness like
a broken attempt at
love of the body
huddled together
on the blue carpet
in the living room of this
in the city
streets long enough
to get lost in yourself again
a glimpse at reality
never finding love
again
and into something

Penelope at Rest
Stanley Galloway

Twenty years collapsed into a single night –
a blink reveals
loathsome suitors gone
the torment of the hall now silent and
the figment who had fathered dear Telemachus now flesh
the memory alive like mist made into man.

I half believe the stories could be true he tells
long into the night
but only when the final flicker sleeps and
and on the steadfast bed he built
in the darkness of a splinter moon
I dare to touch
like blind Tiresias at first
his bicep   and his once-familiar belly
cautious that this isn't yet another trick of
goddess or deceptive god
his body says, *It's really me*
in silent language lovers know but can't explain
and once my palm perceives his beating heart
my body replies
despite the hurt of silent years
loosening the wetness I thought lost to youth
murmuring *I've missed you more than you can know.*

His body answers in the dark –
breathing softer than the storytelling bursts
he'd used to woo me once again –
the way his shoulder curls beneath my neck,
his arm along my naked back,
my breasts divided
                    one atop his chest and
                one
                        beside
and all unbidden my left leg acute across his groin.
The aptness of the feel
latent in me

46

unpracticed in the decades of his absence
says more than any thousand vows.

I tickle-tangle fingers in the hairs
now silvered on his chest,
tugging out the silent plea:
assure me now without your words
by the safety of your arms
  the sureness of your weight
  the satisfaction of your body
  whispering into my heart I'm home to stay.

Somehow Lost / Dreaming of a Future / I Am Wondering If / Extraterrestrial
A. Logan Hill

x

somehow lost
in the forgotten sunset,
huddled in the
crouched position
like a lover
in the backseat
of a
blooming car
we are the forgotten
wonder of this,
gold streaks
left in the sky
like matches.

x

dreaming of a future
where everything that is not
is not negated,
& where nothing is a
modifier for
something else,
& sky of words
what language,
tell me how important it is
to lose something,
& tell me how unimportant it is
to get you back.
it is something
of the smell
in the underbrush
of roses that
wishes for you,
like you

for something
which is this,
like this
something
i wish for you
& i wish for you
& i wish for you

x

I am wondering if
at somepoint
she'll stop laughing.
please stop laughing,
it's driving me mad.
no one ever said to you
anything funny and yet
there you go,
here we go again,
there you go,
here you go
mademoiselle,
would you like some tea?
sometimes i wonder
if it will ever stop
this madness,
the silent laughter—
maybe if you smile real big
like the half of an orange slice,
or
stop laughing
so we can smoke marijuana
& get high
& go dancing sometime,
like they used to
in the movies

or at the lake
or in the studio
when it's raining
& we can't
take our convertible
on a drive
through the penetrating forest of leaves
& no more rhododendron blooms
 to line the path
& no more weed
in plastic bottles
& no more songs
& no more music
from the restaurant
whiskey until
you find
her

x

extraterrestrial
indigenous
landscapes
a foreign body
part human
part fish
the part that is human
indigenous
& the part that is fish
a foreign body,
not human,
our bodies
extraterrestrial
between
breaths.

The Last Affair of Mind

Sirwan Kajjo

This silence inside of us
is so pervasive that it
has peeled off the skin
 of our senses.
The intensity of this silence
is lethal,
and I find that compelling.

The shreds that once
belonged to us
are scattered all over
our exhausted memories.
They collide with the stubbornness
of our little heads.

This silence inside of us
is static and incredibly passive.
It kills the moment with
fear,
panic,
and confusion.
It mutes the motions that
desire to utter their subdued
schemes.

Sometimes being unable to speak
the necessary is
the necessity per se.

Empty Cars
Dawn Leas

You walk into the kitchen,
shaking the February cold
from your coat,
flecks of snow melt in your hair.

I stir a pot of sauce, its steam carries past Sunday
dinners at my parents', kids playing Go Fish

in the family room. You lean against the island
and cross your arms. I'm slicing cloves of garlic

when you say that empty cars, dark and idle,
in the driveway, make you sad sometimes.

I stop chopping and for the first time since the boys left,
I see you, really know you. I no longer question

what keeps a marriage together through years of northern
winters, no sun, only grey clouds, slick ice,

what moves people past the fringe into longing again.

"Empty Cars" first appeared in *San Pedro River Review.*

Consequence
Andrew Manyika

An Hourglass!
A Pair of Wayfarers!
A Chalice!

Hold the image, as the tale of the untold damage
Done to a wax-winged bird, bold in plumage unfolds
She plummets
As she drifts on the ocean, tossed here by the winds of reason,
And there by the waves of emotion
She tweets, to no avail
Tries to speak, but does not prevail
And as the tide breaks, she washes ashore,
She's beached without a sail.

We don't outgrow wanting to be touched.

And she had never needed it so much
As she did whilst she waited on the silent sound to say that she could fly again
She lies in the sand and made a mattress of the grains
With many hours passed, she stands at last
And shakes those grains into her hourglass. And turns it.
This is how her time amongst us begins.
She has forsaken the form of the creature with broken wings,
The bird has blossomed and become a human,
Better yet, she has chosen the way fairer form
She has become, a woman.
In the meantime,
I put on my wayfarers, and step to the stage,
Because I am a rapper and I spit with a rage,
I scream, I say, "I'm ill!
& I can only get iller.
Ladies know love doesn't get much realer
Than in the arms of a legitimate lady-killer.
I'm like a lion in wait but I pounce like Godzilla!"
As I step of stage something brings her to my field of vision.
As we speak it clicks that she's here because she followed the links to my site.
So I proceed to bind her to myself with a chain made of links to my sight.

I take my glasses off and let her in, the hourglass turns.
This is how our time together begins.

Months pass and as we stand after I've caught her,
It strikes me how she's such a lamb to the slaughter
A sheep in the big city, or
As she puts it, "pig city"
We're stagnant, static, but the electricity
Activates her sexually
And with my wayfarers on I try to sell myself this illusion
That her way is fairer on a road with me, but I'm disillusioned
Because love or piety won't let me be a Pharisee
Given how I far I see, I recognise the truth and abandon the players
doctrine
And without getting a doctor in
I diagnose her heart's condition, in love.
Try to stop her before she starts the mission, I'm late
So before this becomes the tale of a tragic blossom,
I pull her aside and try to explain to her that "dammit!
Due to the former exploits of what I thought was my "magic" Johnson,
I'm ill, and I can only get iller.
And yes I know, love doesn't get much realer
But if you choose me you make me a literal lady-killer
What's eating me is lying in wait,
But will pounce on you like Godzilla."
But it's like she's not listening.
It's like she's playing at picking Pokémon, pointing her finger at me and
saying,
"Godzilla...! I choose you."

The paradox of the innocent bystander
Is that there is no innocence in standing by

So I'm guilty
Of not driving home the point
that due to what we've done,
We're warming ourselves with fires from the cool side of the sun,
We're still burning. and her eyes are churning.
And in trying to trace the trajectory of her tears I lose my way
Because they're lost in the laughter lines still lingering around her lips
She's smiling.

We don't outgrow wanting to be touched,
But sometimes what we don't choose, is by whom, where and how much.
I touched her heart and it splintered.
She takes two shards, with the first
She clips her own wings and chooses to become earthbound
She abandon making bird-sound
With the second
She cuts a hole through the hourglass and turns it
And we watch our time running out.
Finally empty, the hourglass becomes our glass, a chalice
From which we both take sips,
It's an act of love done without malice,
But as we do it, all dreams of the future,
Are born, dance and die in the mingling of our now mangled lips.

Soul Mate
Michelle O'Hearn

Thank you for giving me hope for my day
I woke up this morning and it wasn't to play
I've got to be there sometime around eight
I just don't want to hear them hand down my fate.

But after talking to you, I can see clear
That I don't want to spend these hours in fear
I'd rather take this time just sitting here
With you holding my hand, kissing my ear.
And when I get there and they give me two years
Please don't start asking yourself why you're still here.

And if you don't mind, I'd like to ask why
You spend your nights awake not trying to cry
I'll understand and you don't have to lie
I might be ill but I am here by your side.

And when these two years have passed and I'm gone
You have my blessing to live life and move on.
Just think of me watching you from above
And all those hot nights we spent making love.

Thank you for giving me hope for my day
You were my joy, my happiness all the way
You were my true love, my only soul mate
And I'll be waiting for you here by The Gate.

And if you don't mind, I'd like to ask why
You spend your nights awake still trying to cry.
I'll understand and you don't have to lie
I might be gone but I'm still here by your side.

The Shimmering Blacktop of My Spine
Sarah Elizabeth Murphy

The hot scent
of hyacinth,
heavy
glow
of candlelight
hanging
pendulum
weighing
what is
to come.

The heart,
filled to the chambers
with love;
exultation
of
you,
and you,
and you.

Bring
that star shine,
Universal attractant
setting
the mind at ease
and spirit
on fire.

You are heat,
singing
body electric
singed
on the tip of the tongue.
A match stick,
put out
between licked fingers.

You are strange,
foreign,
some fruit
I don't know
how to eat,
but wishing
I could taste.

Once,
I caught your bouquet.
I would dare
to do it again,
laying down
volumes,
thickening desire,
heat and emotion
on the shimmering
blacktop of my spine.

I Have My Doubts
Sarah Elizabeth Murphy

I've had to pass through
Roadblocks,
checkpoint strikeforce,
Homeland Security,
to look into the depths of your eyes.
And now I have headaches,
neck held stiff from gazing,
emotions wound
so tightly
I could burst into tears
at any given moment.
And still I can't reach you;
let alone whisper my words
of softness,
of longing,
of depth
and desire.
I am frozen,
iced,
like some
cubic measurement
of time that I
can not,
nor ever will be.
These words are electric;
they echo round my skull,
rattling the chambers of my heart.
I am alive,
with no intention of wasting
my breath waiting in line.
I left everything I knew
to walk these few steps
closer to you.

Never knowing
what could have been,
for what may never be.
Like those that cross the borders
leaving for something better,
what it is
remaining to be seen.

Sugar Babe
Anna Lena Phillips

"Ain't got no use for your red rocking chair
Got no sugar honey baby there"　　　—Dock Boggs

Soon you will eat summer peaches and be content;
first, crush rabbit tobacco between your fingers.
To think of him at all is time ill-spent—
let bark beetles scrawl across a widow-maker.

Crush rabbit tobacco between your fingers
and let its fragrance blur the scent of him.
In bark beetles' scrawl across a widow-maker
you'll find no trace remaining of his name.

Let another fragrance blur the scent of him.
Watch fishes' scales gleam silver sentences—
you'll find no trace remaining of his name;
its syllables lift from your mind like mist off ice.

Watch fishes' scales gleam silver sentences;
pour vinegar over the songs you sang with him—
syllables lift from your mind like mist off ice.
"Ain't got no use" was made to be sung alone.

Pour vinegar over the songs you sang with him.
But before you erase him, send him green persimmons—
"Ain't got no use" was made to be sung alone—
to turn his mouth inside out: reverse the kiss.

Before you erase him, send him green persimmons.
To remember him at all is time ill-spent—
turns the mouth inside out, reverses the kiss.
Sit down. Eat summer peaches. Be content.

"Sugar Babe" first appeared in *Poemeleon*.

Naked Childhood
John Saleh

In my country, children dream of the open air
With their fingers, they draw schools and toys in the sky.
They write their songs with a naked innocence.
They furnish the snow to make beds for themselves.
They sleep under a sky full of warplanes
 and barrel bombs.
A little girl holds the remaining of a blind bullet
 in her palms.
A boy attempts to remember the face of his mother who
was buried under the ruins of their bombed house.
This boy was grown ahead of his age.
He was part of the war-and-peace game.
He learned the alphabet of freedom in the morning.
And at the end
of the day, the boy drowned in a pool
and his little dreams
remained unachieved in the silence of the place.
In my country, children disappear in to
the legends of freedom.
They transform into birds,
they transform into rain,
they transform into stories.
But there is still hope… and there is still light.

The Stages of Love
Albert Russo

diaphanous blue
cloven by the Eiffel Tower
in your virgin space

a veil of dust
draping my body
the sound of your breath

velo di polvere
vestendo il mio corpo
il tuo respiro

iridescent dot
sucked into a chalice
flower tongues ladybug

the moment your lips meet
you can kiss friendship goodbye
the flesh takes over

bocca a bocca
non è più amicizia
la carne vince

skin against skin
and the magic operates
till the cells rebel

the difference between
a sex maniac and a lover
body temperature

la differenza tra
maniaco ed amante
temperatura

beware dear lovers
passion is a clash of wills
bound to implode

he fell in love with her,
but she looked elsewhere, smitten,
his heart a gaping wound

s'innamoro di lei
senza rendersi conto
solitudine

My Understanding of Love from a Man—or— The Rubber Boy (born the same year as I, 1979)

A reconstructed text from Marc Hartzman's *American Sideshow*

Nicelle Davis

Straitjacket routine done backwards—
he first did it to be cheeky—to lose his
job. Now, he is famous for escapes into
restraint: *The World's Only Living
Enterologist.*

Self Discovery: Age 4, he fell
from his bunk-bed and landed split
in half. Then books with pictures.
Contortion. Mimicry as hobby.

Final act: Dislocates hips and shoulders.
Carefully rearranges ribs. Drops heart
below sternum. So an audience can
watch his heart beating.

My Understanding of Love of Self—or—
What I Can Recall from the Film
The New Sideshow
Nicelle Davis

Lucyfire says,

I ask the audience if they want blood. Always
the answer is *Yes*. Until bleeding—
then they all yell
No, no.

The act in summary is this:

With a syringe she pours herself into a cup
and drinks. She makes this look like
hunger's first contact with
consumption—lips so
erect you can see
her mouth
pulsing.

Lucyfire says,

I had a normal childhood, maybe spent
too much time alone
with a book—
of matches.

Commandments of Fingers
John Saleh

Be free with no shackles.
The fetters of the moment and this place
make me love you even more.
They make me prepare my horses
to look for your winds.

After a while, I will get out
of my coffin and remove the silence
from my body.
I will walk the streets naked without
the fig leaf and the masks of fear.
I will hold my red poems and with them,
I will decorate the entrances of
this forgotten city.
From here they had passed... the tyrants of history
but they had forgotten that rain cleanse traces of
the streets every year.

My grandmother says: God is with you...
Be free and never bow.

Today I just learned why my friends
are lofty - like the oak – when they climb
the walls of our country.
Their shadows are longer than
the batons of the police.
Their fingers learn
the alphabet of hope and freedom.

Wonderland Alic'd *(for Mumia)*
Amoja Sumler

The action of this poem spills fluid;
bondage
from those that demand debts
paid on time
or see me Wonderland Alice'd
(in chains)
wrong(ly convicted).

The action of this poem is daggers

misprinted lies,
begging for the policeman's
angry baton again
and again
because
bloody and beaten means I'm still breathing;
it's something to feel;
it's better than dead.

The action of this poem is the violence
of our empty
hands punching
only sky
when the Blue man group
dare us
"Freeze"
painting us
still death
their medium: lead
screaming to me from somewhere
quick as a fifteen year old's erection.

Brothers try and hope.
They've lost their minds.
The vision of this poem is grungy
blurry as Seattle skies
moist as the mud's soaking

up potential measured in the blood of hood boys
up to no good boys.

Are you like me?
Confused?
You don't understand
who they
thought I was
supposed to be:
darkness incarnate,
the motherfucking devil,
a reflection of their fears,
a million men marching
dressed like Nat Turner
transported through time
armed like Ferguson army cops.

Am I wrong?
I'd like to fly
but it's alright.

No excuses,
I know that pain and I won't run away
(like I used to do).

Every day
a bad day.

Hands are bruised from
breaking rocks.
I'm one of the lucky ones
(something's gotta turn out right).

The action of this
poem is the victory
of my lungs still full,
my pants unsoiled, body

still hiding from angry chair

'cause Life Drinker stay thirsty.

Little boy made a mistake,
dissenting loud enough to be heard.

Here they come as the rooster crows
and the pig dies.

Why'd it have to be this way?
They say the killer is me.

Get on your knees! Time to pray!
Boy!
Do what you want to do.
Direct your fate (it's over now).

The action of this poem is the glare
of guards training AR-15's
down in a hole.

The locale is the place where weakness
gets you fucked in the ass so
I will speak no more
of my feelings,
except to say
(corporate prison we stay)

America: I want to
be inside of you
losing my soul;
a flower with wide brown eyes that blooms in your tomb,
out of control,
like the weed you planted,
but not smoked like the others.

Please consent to hold me here.

water cure: *a telegraph to 1901 from the future*
Aimee Suzara

Get the good old syringe boys and fill it to the brim

lifesource our liason to the sea lessoned on insurgents stop

attempt to get confession force the feel of drowning stop

cause waterlung/pneumonia cause pleuritis cause adrenaline overload cause irregular heart beat cause release of catecholamines cause heart attack stop

proven despite CIA sanitation of a formal method yes one can be scared to death stop

We've caught another n------- and we'll operate on him

if not from broken limbs or bruises if not oxygen loss if not vital organ failure stop

and under this distress one will admit to anything stop

post interrogation should one survive now fear the gentle sprinkle on a rainy day a pool a shower anything aquatic stop

administration and united nations deem it form of torture stop

Shouting the battle cry of freedom

stop
stop
stop

wonder who the terrorist is

*Text in italics from a U.S. Army marching song written during the Philippine-American War.

This poem is reprinted from *Souvenir* (WordTech, 2014).

The Rose City of Petra
Albert Russo

Behind the mount of Hor
where Aaron is buried
in the Valley of Moses
the Nabateans
built palaces of splendor
carved in the rock
lofty canyons scraping
the sky of a limpid
translucent blue
Surrounded by the desert
a thousand walls
sprout in phantasmal hues
from sand pink to coal brown
through all the shades of coral
defying the laws of gravity
Walking in the narrow corridors
that separate them
you feel at once dwarfed and exhilirated
imagining you are
the emissary of a foreign court
awaited by the King of Petra
And the towering walls
stand guard, protecting you
all the way to the palace
Then all of a sudden
as if emerging from a dream
between the cracks of a gorge
a doric column appears
holding parts of
a monumental crown
An ethereal silence sets in
and you slow your pace
lest the miracle fades into a mirage
the air is brimming
with sand particles
yet you fear that
if you remain still

you will be turned
into a pillar of salt
like Lot's wife in the Bible
your feet shuffle
on the pebbly ground
and the crunching sound
fills you with terror
then in a surge of courage
you slip out of the crack
and face the majestic facade
of the golden Khaznah

Puja
Joshua Gray

The priest throws holy water on the crowd
as we pray among the scent of incense smoke.
The moon hears a heavy bell on the temple porch.
Hinduism is not a religion, it is a philosophy.

In the worshipping room, Kali goddess of black death
looks on, tongue out, stiff as stone, blood-stained.
Like art galleries, more worship rooms in adjacent places
praise Ganesha, others. I wish to be a chameleon. But

this is her week: the moon and sun alike chant
to the mother goddess wife of Siva in all her forms.
We consume her blessings from banana leaf plates and clay cups.
Hinduism is not a religion, it is a way of life.

Performers dance and sing and romp, all under a tented stage,
all dedicated to Durga. As we surround the performers
and flail around with the dancers we witness the art
of flower giving, priest worshipping, food offerings, tabla drumming.

In its final act the crowd of thousands parades through black veins
toward the deified river, holding high wax icons of divine motherhood,
the sun beating down hard, to where it dunks its idols
into waxing waters polluted with borne illnesses.

"Puja" was originally published in *Zombie Poetry*.

Seasonal Yarns of Slum Dwellers
Susil Mandal

Seasonal yarns of slum dwellers
Cross the door-sill of a cubicle
To roll on the stained floor of another.
The blunt slicer raises its face
Toward the slice of sky visible through the tattered roof.
Lying beside the slicer a buxom dalit woman-
How many times the slicer scraped her throat!
In this cubicle the male honeymoons with liquor.

Sometimes the rain-drenched hour
Erects dreams of connubial bliss;
The refugee wife
Feels shockwaves of desire in her secret chambers.
Her drunken man, on that hour,
Revels in erotic shrieks of another woman
Behind the pall of ruffled darkness;
In the same inferno- the only inferno for the damned.

Translated by Indranil Acharya
The original Bengali poem titled "Bastir Ghargulir Morshumi Galpo"
was included in *Anuchyar Taranga*, an anthology published by Dey's
Publishing, Kolkata, in 2010.

Ayla
Susil Mondal

On the bustling road
Procession of countless heads sans banners and slogans;
The rickety fingers desperately clutch at relief food grains
With the surging tides of discontent.
Those who clamoured for drinking water
Now groan in acute pain of thirst—
Towering demon of thirst in sweltering heat.
The newborn babe was devoured by
The predator flush flood—
The iron-clasp of a resilient mother
Failed to save it.
Now she whispers in profound delirium
Untold elegies of colossal waste.

Translated by Indranil Acharya

The original Bengali poem titled "Bhater Gandho" was included
in *Anuchyar Taranga*, an anthology published by Dey's Publishing,
Kolkata, in 2010.

Aroma of Rice

Susil Mondal

While walking on the road the man dreams of rice.
Sometimes chapattis cross his dream;
But at times, the unborn child of his carrying wife
Make him sink in dire distress.
In the forty years of his pigmy life
He has not seen a bowl full of rice five times.
Yet he has cogitated on a sumptuous meal a thousand times;
How passionately he would gorge on his favourite bowl of rice!

When the *Krishnachura* ignites the whole summer day
With its fiery red hue – this man suffers from a burning stomach;
He has visited many doctors and faith-healers for cure.
But all are unanimous on one remedy—
It's not a bowlful of rice;
Before his death, he can at most fill in
His sunken lungs with a strong aroma of rice.

Translated by Indranil Acharya

The original Bengali poem titled "Bhater Gandho" was included
in *Anuchyar Taranga*, an anthology published by Dey's Publishing,
Kolkata, in August, 2010.

A Tale of Rice and Full Moon

Susil Mondal

When we were exploring
The heights of pleasure
Their life was darkened
By the craving for a bowl of rice.
When we were cruising
On a speed boat in the deep sea
And dwelling mutely on the rhyme of the seas
They were cocooned in their tiny huts
And waiting for a new morn
With a sea of hunger eddying within.
When on a moonlit night
We were sailing on a river
With thousand memories of smouldering passion
They risked their lives amidst
Crocodiles and tigers
To earn a bowl of rice and dreams.
As they throng in thousands
Beneath the *Shahid Minar* for a rally,
We watch the commotion for a bowl of rice
On *Star Ananda* and cling
To our monsoon flicks.
As they get drenched
By the smart shower and wait
We gorge on the delicious *hilsa*
And belch in a post-lunch bliss.

Translated by Indranil Acharya

The original Bengali poem titled "Bhat ebong Jyotsnar Galpo" was
included in *Anuchyar Taranga*. an anthology published by Dey's
Publishing, Kolkata, in 2010.

Simulacra

Joani Reese

Men drag the last wild woman from her home concealed above a
verdigris-tipped sea. A gag secures her mouth; red thread sews closed
labial folds. They cuff her hands behind her back and dangle golden
keys from chains around their necks. They truck her over the pass
to the flatlands, all colors muted green and gray. Pain curls her like a
question mark as tamed women bend her bones into the cage where she
complies, or dies.

Men blunt her claws, excise her teeth, attack until her mind succumbs.
They dress her up; they dress her down. Her face is tattooed with a
smile, her womb unlaced, perfectly numbed. She learns to kneel in
darkness all her own. Each year evolves into the next. A zealous drab,
she sates with sex; she gestates younger, pliant girls, then teaches each to
ape a paper doll.

Maldegem, 1963, 1993
William Sypher

In Flanders fields
rows and rows of future
long-stemmed roses
stretched half a mile.
No mercantile sense,
they grew amiss, not at ends
of long, straight stems,
the popular persuasion.

They needed grafting and we signed on,
my college chum and I, on summer leave
working alongside Belgian men
in blue coveralls and sashes,
and wooden shoes
that made sucking sounds in the mud.

Little more than stand-ins
dressed in city clothes,
still we played the part;
rode five miles on decrepit bikes
down wet-brown lanes,
through puddles, to the fields,

In teams of five
we bobbed like fishing corks
along the timeless rows,
bending down to slit the roots,
fitting them with fresh-cut buds,
then standing up to slice more buds
from branches in a pouch
strung 'round our waist.
Then down again to slit and fit.
up and down, up and down,
endless, timeless rows.
Let Van Gogh freeze this scene in time--
we dared not freeze
our backs in place, and so

we bobbed the summer long.
At times, we stopped
when clods of dirt
came whistling by our ears,
fusillade from a nearby team
begging us to break the tedium:
bending, standing, bending, standing.
The battle joined, the air was clogged
with clods of dirt and clouds of dust,
grunts from heaving, threats and laughter,
ending only when our arms grew tired,
or when the rumble of an old Mercedes
meant field boss Roget was near.
He would have the roses primed
for flower stalls in Brussels.
War games were not his fancy.
No clods flew by his ears.

When Roget rumbled out of sight
the team resumed its glacial pace.
My friend and I, American-true
would show our working mates
we hadn't come to play:
one hundred grafts an hour,
then one fifty
and a hundred more.
We forged ahead,
as if it were a race.
A clod or two aimed at our heads
reset the glacial pace.

In a hut we ate our lunch
and there the games resumed.
Antoine, red-haired and apple-cheeked,
self-appointed jester,
never tired of peeling oranges
in one continuous spiral.
Then clicking on his lighter,

he squeezed the oily peel into the flame,
bringing forth a fiery stream that
pleased him and the others daily.
Anlar laughed the loudest.

Except for Antoine, busy shooting flames,
we sat inside the hut, on benches.
Antoine chose a pole stuck in the ground
a pole two inches round.
We could not fathom his nonchalance
or such a steely bottom.

Anlar, maybe 45, and grinning
gap-toothed, several neurons missing,
daily hid his bag lunch
in the woods beside the field,
daily shrieked to find it
ruined by a fellow worker
who had relieved himself.
It was but another game, however cruel.
Anlar didn't know the rules,
didn't want to play.

One day I, too, walked into the woods
for relief, not to play the Anlar game,
and came upon some unexploded bombs,
dozens of them, all alike with rounded ends
lying calmly, dangerously among the trees
beside the fields of roses.
I sat on one and ate my lunch
hoping that a bomb which lay there
undisturbed for twenty years
would not awake and add another victim
to the War which caused us
then to number wars
so we could keep the carnage straight.

At day's end we aimed our bikes for home
up muddy lanes and down the asphalt road.
The Flanders wind scoured our faces
no matter what the weatherman had said.

We dived into the wind which bent
the trees to forty-five degrees.
and made our trip uphill, it seemed.
Determined not to let it bend us
more than the fields could bend us
we fought our way home--

Home? More pointedly, a mansion:
we dined on crystal, slept on silk,
befitting the cousin from America
and his college friend.
This transfiguration, from daytime serf
to evening bourgeoisie, unsettled us
as we left the house each morning,
walking 'cross the graveled yard
filled with real, full-time field hands
who gaped at our good fortune.

In August, we flew home from it all
back to academic games,
back to our authentic selves.
In Maldegem, oranges still spurt flames
and roses still grow straight and tall.

1993

Three decades on, now father of three,
it dawned on me to show them
where I'd worked and lived
when I was young and ripe for change,
enough of oral history.

By train and languorous bus,
four hours from the North of France
I couldn't wait to show my girls
fields of roses, rows
that stretched so far
you could no longer see
what people paid for.
Each row which started red or pink
faded into black and white

half a mile away.
Van Gogh was right.

Comforting landmarks were gone.
I could not find the street,
not even the tiny pub
where I had first drunk cola warm,
and collected Stella Artois coasters
like a witless tourist.

"DeKonick-Dervais Nursery?"
I asked the round-faced postal clerk
who pointed to the east.
Closure was at hand for me,
now my girls could see
the place where I'd been shaped
by summer work,
my first time in the Old World.

We walked five blocks and I could see
the multi-gabled, red brick home
which had transmuted me each night
from field hand to landed man,
where I had dined on coq au vin
talked of Van Eyck, Sartre and JFK.
The sight of the old home
jolted cobwebbed memories;
at last I could present my past.

As we drew near, my fever cooled,
my shoulders sagged.
Once well-kept lawns
grew high in weeds,
weathered plywood filled
each window frame.
The nursery had grown amok.
Graceful, long-stemmed roses
had been ousted by wild flowers,
sturdy peasant stock
which needed no grafting
by any lads in coveralls.

The cultivated life was at an end;
wild nature had reclaimed the land.
The family had grown old, I learned,
the children yearned more for Brussels' lights
than for rows of long-stemmed roses.

Thirty years--I should have known--
how could I think it would go on?
So I could show my girls my rustic past?
Ha, it was a job,
a summer lived, not painted.
I had worked in a field,
not a museum
and my life had been so ripe
with blossoms and with grafting of my own,
I had not grasped
how much time had passed.

Thirty years is long enough to tire
of selling long-stemmed roses
in flower stalls in Brussels.

Luggage
Justin Walmsley

I AM shaking
beside a second beside dust
carrying luggage toward that next second
notice. Seconds falling ghastly on platforms
platforms carrying dust in droves for carnal insects themselves a herd

memory is so trapezoid against dominoes
flick,   grit,   tag,   bicycle   wheel,   baseball cards
taped together taped to it
rattling as rattle through neighborhoods
        through rooms who truly room, train cars and dining cars and
caboose

people speak too easily and ask narcissistic questions
holding, in drug frenzy, their waists or champagne
healthy and morose and happy at once
once falling naked in sand
each tiny sphere sticking not to skin because of sweat,
but cheap moisturizer that evolves into lovers caught in trees and alleys
fools becoming fools with ideals followed by trails of moist toilettes
like tolls for booths erected on the failed and decayed souls of personas
personas with lovely parents and there!!
…a giant clock framed in ironwork as dainty as are the flourishes in the
finest chyna
belonging to the family you are currently running from

veterans slaying floors containing luggage
floors severing orphans from orphans

I Suppose
Angela M. Carter

I suppose I wore a little thing of a dress many times that summer,
my long, disproportioned legs making the hem fall too short.
In fairness, when I was asked what I did to deserve the attention,
no words built upon my tongue to amount to any reason.
Guilty, I was,
my echo of memory still remains a slur.

I suppose I laughed too heavily, snorts and all,
spit fell under my bottom lip as I did.
I thought I should love even if hesitant
because you sat up straight only when he came around.
Your lips became feminine and loose and would make it closer to
my forehead;
they never fully landed.

The acting,
the bruises,
the "she" taken from the inside, the "it" of me
never pained me as much as the silence that followed.
It is my skin that I have shed
but my mind that has grown layers of nonflowering seeds that
even I can't seem to profit from.

I suppose because I was old before I was young
I've silently given men permission to take my skin as their hide.
The beat of worry and damaged goods easily detected
in advance
to their plan of breaking me apart anyway.
Validation, to the hunter, I breathe.

What began as a back rub one afternoon
became the front rub,
became drilled holes in the walls for easy view,
became doors that would not lock,
became cars that could not be driven,
became me yelling out loud in pastures of no scenery,
became me being pulled into the backseat of a school bus and

shushed
when I told the principal and the teacher about the boy,
became me losing my tongue,
playing dead until there was nowhere to play anymore.

I suppose I did long to be wanted,
liked it when anyone ran their nails softly over my scalp and ear,
relished the way some listened to me,
but don't we all when we know of nothing that could happen beyond?

Older Boys
Dawn Leas

She always liked older boys –

last names ending in vowels,
Irish Whiskey for blood,
WASP, Catholic, a Jew,
Blonde curls, receding hairlines,
dark chocolate eyes, dazzling green.

But the first one, a neighborhood kid
with basketball legs, found her,
tented a blanket, polyester rubbing
against her scabbed knees.

When he said it was just like a doctor's
visit, she stared at her Raggedy Ann,
arms and legs splayed on orange shag.

His breath on her legs,
she turned to Sesame Street
songs on the console TV, a beacon
just out of reach.

His hands pushed open her thighs,
the tent became a fort
built for Pop Tarts
and Saturday morning cartoons –
a canopy of ruby leaves,
a spider web on dewy grass,
clouds shaped like ocean waves.

Back in the den, it was a mine shaft –
crumbling walls, sagging beams,
layers of coal dust.

Far beneath the surface
words got lost in the dark.
So much land on her shoulders,

she felt the good air leaving,
odorless gas rising and like a canary,
she learned the ways of silence.

"Older Boys" was originally published in *Everyday Escape Poems* (SwanDive Publishing, 2014).

The Long Look
Lynne Thompson

—this boy I am remembering
        put his eyes on me—

he stepped out of his body
and let it pool around his ankles
        like a lagoon—

        He put his eyes on me

and they were shameless—

less rapacious than cling

        and shadow

and I must have looked like an icon
or a victim:

        arms, waist, shoulders
and their blades, butt and kneecaps
all of me   an improbable bargain

Still, he didn't take his eyes away—

just let them unbend   then open

        like envelopes

        while he inhaled

looked at my wrist and heels and
any other part of my anatomy
he had not yet oppressed—

Darkly, my flesh turned

and my skin, wanting, spoke:

        don't   please
but he wasn't finished—

.

the fortune of wombs
Aimee Herman

She turned her face into a bundle of tumbleweeds. *Good luck*, she grunted from between cave of toothless mouth.

It is Thursday and clothes commit suicide in nearby laundromat on Utica Avenue in Brooklyn. The drown is purchased with plastic card, dipped into metal machine meant to take the dirt away.

Two doors down, you press brown boots over blue carpet in pharmacy where everything exists behind locked glass and nothing is permitted a touch.

Can I have a pregnancy test, you ask with unrehearsed syllables.

She looks at the creases of queer giving you away. Price ranges from fourteen dollars to almost thirty and you wonder if some things should not be bargained down like antibiotics or plastic meant to determine your future fertility.

You collected your urine all morning inside a bladder that has grown used to this sort of mistreatment.

When the laundry dries out, you walk one and a half blocks with keys between fingers. You approach door with glass stained into it, and unlock it. Your clothes drop onto your bed, which is smoothed out and removed of last night's haunt. No one is home in this moment, so you leave the bathroom door open as you remove your pants.

Fabric fumbles at your ankles and is soon joined by your underwear, color of the shadow that has followed you since childhood. You are fairly certain that directions are not necessary to read, but you squint your eyes over them regardless.

Place box on sink, unwrap stick and place between legs.

As you free the yellow from your bladder (color confiding in you that perhaps you need to drink more water), the liquid slaps against the stick. You count to five and keep going. The last number you hear yourself speaking is twenty-four, the age you were the first (and last) time you engaged in this movement.

As you wait for a line to tell you what exists inside your womb, you jump inside the shower. Here, the water ~~scolds~~ scalds your skin.

In five minutes you decide on abortion. Contemplate the name Eleanor or Casey. Calculate the cost of stamps through long-distance correspondence once they are old enough to ask whom their *real* mother is.

Your skin is drizzled with worry and wet. A towel—dyed from the lies that color your hair—wraps itself around you as you carefully approach the plastic stick.

One line will let you know you are the only one inside your body.

Two lines will alert you that another has gained entrance.

Your eyes blink open. Your skin drips. You are still alone.

How to live paycheck to paycheck
Dawn Leas

Always wear hot-pink scrubs on Mondays,
        holidays and for monthly staff meetings.
Remain calm when your co-worker calls off
        with a full waiting room at 7:05 a.m.
Cradle the phone on your shoulder
        as you place ID stickers on vials
        and tell your daughter she can not
        wear shorts to school in December
        on a day forecasted for snow.
Sing Peter Gabriel's *Red Rain*
        while inputting diagnostic codes
        into the computer.
Slide the needle in effortlessly
        while telling the patient she is lucky
        to have a 14-vial doctor,
        one who wants to know why.
Unknot tourniquet one-handed,
        switch full vial for new one
        when explaining daughter's
        gifts this year are on layaway
        winter coat, school clothes,
        one video game –
        That's it.
Apply pressure to stop the bleeding
        and when gauze soaks red, assure
        the patient – yourself – it will stop, eventually.

semi-colon
Aimee Herman

:::   ::::::::::::::::::::::   ;   :::::::::::::::
:::::::::::::::::::::   ::

It is more than just a curve and elevated moon   lingering
without string or staircase. Call it an in-   visible
floatation device. It separates and splits;   there
       is an aroma of two within each *one*. Call it semi-colon;
       see it as asymmetrical complexity. Punctuated
       human.

Perforated skin arrives for comments and question marks. When nudity
gathers, globular organs gaze at external biological cues. Must there be a
need for clarity. Exist within abstraction and rummaged investigations.
Call gender: *voyage* or *crusade.*

How about you hike your way toward the peak of these bones &
translate the echo that accelerates back.

I am in-between the sentence-structure of my
body ; two independent clauses ; flattened raw on one
    side and hairy and grey and elephant and embodied
    and wouldn't it be easier if the forms were less con-
        constructed and wouldn't it be best if we could just
exist within the ellipses of our bones.

How to persist within measurements and the texture of genetics.
Genitals are animalistic and acoustic. Call them reverb. Work your way
out of sleepy veins. Sculpt a word for this third gender contemplation
into something else not called male but   *human* or *breathing.*

Some of what hangs, sparkles. Call these drag
routines. Hair is just an arrival of death grow-
ing from life drenched with peroxides and scissors.
Call yourself a planet because all this
space derives from punctured cells and this
floatation device called gender is permitting you to

wander now.   Or *wonder* now.

Call body a stoop sale. There may be a need to discount limbs. Half
price on the parts no longer in use and what happens when skin forgets
its cause.

With each person you are with, your body moves dif-   ferently.
There are rules and permits and directions   and
menus. Your body rarely trusts another to under-
stand how to approach it. Some may think they can track
your shapes until you go against the rotation.
So *rotate*.

All of this may be disrupted and you can install a shelving
 unit or rod. And you can call your body a ferris wheel or movie sequel
or thunderbolt or serrated verb or reappraisal or _____ .

Metallurgy
Sarah Elizabeth Murphy

I say I don't believe in soul mates
but that I believe in signs.
My parents alloy
one part practical
one part dreamer
and born from their
collaboration of genes.

I seem to have
forgotten myself,
depressed myself,
transgressed myself.
Spending so much time
running around,
telling myself,
selling myself
forgetting to listen for
that ring of truth.

It's no wonder I want to
turn myself off,
deprogram myself,
examine myself.
Desperately searching
for stress fractures,
malleable metal
turned brittle and frail,
this dream for a new day
turned vapid and stale.

And this skin?
This skin will always stay pale.

Buried beneath flesh,
the heart
burnt arterially
into my arm.
Two halves
soldered together,
broken pieces delivered
to heartache's door
expressly packaged
respected for more.

I Took Nothing

Teresa Mei Chuc

and broke it in half.
As if mocking me,
there was an
even greater
nothing and I
felt myself falling.

I took my falling
and broke it
in half. It did
not stop the falling.
I plunged deeper.

I took this depth
and gathered it,
the darkness
with all of its
stars, and
put it in the wings
of a bat.
I watched it
retreat into
the deepest
of caves
where it screams
and listens to
its voice
returning
from stone walls.

"I Took Nothing" was first published in *Rattle*.

Woman Child
Angela M. Carter

I was the waiter.
I waited for the built-up noise of my one-millionth silence
to be acknowledged.

I was a creator.
I fulfilled their need of risen cheeks
before they could gnaw on the woman child within.

I was the secret-keeper.
Opposite ear permanently closed,
one eye winked it's warnings to passersby.
I was the cleaner.
I rocked heavy, limp bodies.
I hid their liquor bottles before they awakened to my cries.

I was the trusted.
Slammed my self-worth on their *sorrys*.
Keep this secret, they said.

I was the woman child.
The heart, tissue paper thin,
with cement and chains, to protect the skin.

I was the runner.
Born from the fastest beast of life.
I ran before I could crawl.

I am the survivor.
I am the dreamcatcher.
I am anything I choose to be now.

Seaside Heights, 2012
Dawn Leas

My body has held the weight of lives.
Millions of running feet,
first kisses, final break-ups,
girls' nights out, family reunions.
So many sunsets.

My arms are a summer home.
FunTown children squeal,
blinking carnival lights,
carousel music looping.
Teenagers scream when the coaster crests a hill,
snuggle at top of a Ferris Wheel
only murmur of foam and balmy air
between them and the stars.

My legs are sturdy like the trees
that made them, support the grieving
who flock to the intersection
of land and water for a glimpse
of someone no longer here.

Now, in the dark, wind rages,
angry water surges. My body bends
to repeat a decades-old prayer.
Please spare me. Please,
as I feel the old burn of fire,
and remember the rage of a mid-century storm.

In the morning, so much sand
and salty water where yesterday
there was none. My body half-buried,
snapped and strewn. One arm mostly
gone, its coaster a collapsed erector set.

But, my legs still stand.
     I am standing.
          Yes, I am still.

"Seaside Heights, 2012" first appeared in *Everyday Escape Poems* (SwanDive Publishing, 2014).

Pink and Blue
Haley Tennant

I like pink.

I like pink and cute clothes and going
"Awww" when I see puppies or babies.
I like talking for hours on the phone with my best friend about
the hot deals of the new season of clothes that come out,
Or which shade of eye shadow would best highlight my features.
I like being a "girl".

And I am not weak.

I do not hit like I've spent all my time barely lifting a finger
except to paint my nails or dial a number.
I *hit* like after painting those nails with Pink Glitter and Lace,
I lived and breathed and stretched out my muscles.
They are hardened by each day.
I have lifted hay bales on cold winter mornings and
hoisted furniture through someone's house
and then helped them turn all those empty rooms
into a home.
My fists have struck punching bags and blocked any
stray hands that think they have any right to touch

Me.

I will strike with every last bit of fury inside me
at being shunted aside for being
Too feminine
Too kind
Too small
Or too ugly.

I hit like a girl
who will leave you with bruises and a reminder that
I will not fit in the box you want me in,
and I will not give my permission to be treated like
A pretty object,

Or disposable once I've hit
My expiration date on beauty.

I am a person and I think and I will not forget the way you
dismissed me like a child when I got too loud and passionate.
I will not forget the way you wrote off my anger as overreacting
and asked me if it's "that time of the month."
I refuse to endure blind dates who become blind themselves once
I stop giggling at every word that crosses their lips and
start talking about my passions;
the very things that keep me breathing are seen as me talking too much.

Sit down.
Be quiet.
Good girl.

I am not your pet.

I am a woman
and you will hear me roar if you do not give me the same respect
I see handed out like candy to all the men around me.
All those men who obviously have it easy because
they get to like blue and cheer for football teams
or go to midnight releases for video games because
They aren't just faking it to fit in with the guys.

They are expected to be strong every day in order to
support those poor, frail women around them
like collectors of porcelain dolls.
Obviously it is easier for the men because they get to be leaders
and hide their tears even when it feels like their guts are being ripped
out by
Invisible demons.
They can talk and laugh and be loud but not if it's about that feeling stuff
that belongs at sleepovers with pillow fights.
Girls and women trademarked that shit long ago,
And you cannot have it.

Because men have it easier,
my father cannot speak to me like my mother,
and at night when he sits in his recliner in silence
I have to pick out the words that are locked up tight inside his eyes and
guess at what he might
want to say from the
Few that find an escape.

This is not a game of Life.
People don't just come in blue and pink,
This is *Life*.
There are thousands of
shades and hues that mix together to
make up each and every person.
Restricting it to two is a crime against
Every single one of us and
I refuse to be told that I can only like
Pink.

Fashion

Lady Caress

I am fashion
A.K.A the puppeteer
Turning fads into faux pas
And faux pas into fads
Whenever I see fit
Dictating your future
And I have you wrapped around my finger
You buy today
And I change the look tomorrow
And of course like all my puppets you merely follow
You get a job not for bills but for me
As if compliments from peers
Is the food that you eat
You need me
Or at least that's what you think
Living life longing for merely a gaze, a glance, a wink
You match the right shoe
With the right pant
Searching for compliments
Like an oasis amongst desert sands
I am
Fashion
A.K.A the puppeteer
Turning fads into faux pas
And faux pas into fads
Whenever I see fit
Dictating your future
And I have you wrapped around my finger
Who are you without me
Brains has left the game
I judge only by what I see
So attach my strings to your hands and feet
Dance around the stage
You beauty of the week
As long as you look good
Forget what you do
The only legacy worth leaving

Is "ooh isn't she cute"
"oh this old thing"
"200 dollar jeans"
I make sure you look clean
I am
Fashion
A.K.A the puppeteer
So if you're at work; forget that, honey bail
Did you not get the memo: Niemen's has a sale
And you better subscribe to Marie Claire
Forget those bible toting believers
Everything you need is in there
Rule number one
There is no window shopping
Who cares if you spent the rent
Why are you stopping
I write the rules
And you obey
After all you're a puppet for goodness sake
And I my dear
Am fashion, the puppeteer
Turning fads into faux pas
And faux pas into fads
Whenever I see fit
Dictating your future
And I have you wrapped around my finger
So get up
Get out
And go get it
If you've got it honey
spend it!

Names
Teresa Mei Chuc

I am tired of having five different names;
Having to change them when I enter

A new country or take on a new life. My
First name is my truest, I suppose, but I

Never use it and nobody calls me by this Vietnamese
Name though it is on my birth certificate –

Tue My Chuc. It makes the sound of a twang of a
String pulled. My parents tell me my name in Cantonese

is Chuc Mei Wai. Three soft bird chirps and they call
me Ah Wai. Shortly after I moved to the U.S., I became

Teresa My Chuc, then Teresa Mei Chuc. "Teresa" is the sound
Water makes when one is washing one's hands. After my first

Marriage, my name was Teresa Chuc Prokopiev.
After my second marriage, my name was Teresa Chuc Dowell.

Now I am back to Teresa Mei Chuc, but I want to go way back.
Reclaim that name once given and lost so quickly in its attempt

to become someone that would fit in. Who is Tue My Chuc?
I don't really know. I was never really her and her birthday

on March 16, I never celebrate because it's not my real birthday
though it is on my birth certificate. My birthday is on January 26,

really, but I have to pretend that it's on March 16
because my mother was late registering me after the war.

Or it's in December, the date changing every year according to
the lunar calendar – this is the one my parents celebrate

because it's my Chinese birthday. All these names
and birthdays make me dizzy. Sometimes I just don't feel like a

Teresa anymore; Tue (pronounced Twe) isn't so embarrassing.
A fruit learns to love its juice. Anyways, I'd like to be string…

resonating. Pulled back tensely like a bow

Then reverberate in the arrow's release straight for the heart.

"Names" was first published online in *Babel Fruit* and republished in print
in *New Poets of the American West Anthology* (Many Voices Press, 2010)

The Things That Mother Said
R.G. Evans

If venetian blinds hung crooked,
or dishes lay piled in the sink,
if empty shoes sat strewn around the floor,
mother would say
Place looks like a niggershack.
It wasn't, of course. It was ourshack.
Catholicshack. Polackshack.
Leather-strap-to-the-thighshack. Bigotshack.
Ventriloquist of doom, her voice
still follows me through unkempt rooms,
and I have to bite my wooden tongue
to silence her in the ground
where satin must sag sloppily now
inside her casketshack.

Originally published in *Rattle*.

A Visit from my Grandfather
Beth Konkoski

Nights when the wind is strong and memories
steam like cocoa, my grandfather comes

to tell my son he loves him. I have seen him,
no more than a gust, dart behind the curtain

when I come in to check. I pretend
not to notice the smell of his pipe

or the shade of plaid he leaves in the room.
He must have something important to tell,

something antique and great-grandfatherly,
perhaps earned from the varnish and wood

of his history, the many chairs and sideboards
he brought back from their own dead places

in the barns and attics of the North Country.
So I tiptoe away, hoping

my child will one day tell me, the secrets
he heard whispered through the bars of his crib.

Ashes
Dawn Leas

My father was a volcano
spewing lava that night,
tables became timber --
curtains fell, walls crumbled.

My mother was a hummingbird
darting between him and us
wings humming false promises
that evaporated in the heat.

In the next room, my sister and I shared
a double bed like we had shared
our mother's womb, a tangle of legs
and arms, her thumping heart close to mine.
A sliver of light sliced our room
as Mother appeared, then disappeared again.

I folded my arms and blinked
like "I Dream of Jeannie."

In the morning, we tiptoed over rocky
landscape, washed our hands in ashes.
We waited.

"Ashes" was originally published in *I Know When to Keep Quiet*
(Finishing Line Press, 2010).

Roots
Dawn Leas

I'm not made of mountains or valleys.
There's no stench of river mud in my hair
or coal dusting my family albums.
My grandfather played stickball on the streets
of Jersey City, sang an Irish Lullaby to court
my grandmother at St. Patrick's in Elizabeth.
He went to work the brewery line, dormant
hops and barley sprouted in his blood, flowed
freely into our clan. Some turned their backs
on its bitter taste and yeasty smell, in others
it brewed and boiled staining our house
for generations. But, my parents escaped,
flew us far from those shadows. Yes, I
was transplanted several times over on plains
and in a city below sea level before landing
in these mountains. I grew roots here, married
local, cultivated lives, began to call it home
for better or worse.

"Roots" was originally published in *Everyday Escape Poems* (SwanDive Publishing, 2014).

Reconciliation
Dawn Leas

We waded through the bayous of my childhood—
black water, a witch's stew churned below a canopy

of arthritic branches. Veins of cypress and tupelo
were mountains to climb. At ground level, no guide,

only ethereal tendrils of light. No guide, we moved
by touch. Humidity heaved a sigh and mildewed air

squeezed our lungs into spontaneous words.
At midnight, you played notes I hadn't yet heard.

Thrum of jazzy bass migrated from the French
Quarter, mood music for the foreign territory

we were now traversing. In the late hours
of a melancholy night we danced with stillness.

Not worrying about cottonmouth venom, piercing
pain of bite, we swam together day and night,

then day again in those chicory waters deep
enough to tread, face to face, lips close.

By summer's waning days, I learned sometimes
to move forward you must go back.

I'm Going Back to North Carolina
Anna Lena Phillips

"I'm going back to North Carolina"

Sheila Kay Adams

Come home with me and kiss me in bright shade
along the bikeway and creek where muscadine
curls over asphalt and sewer line,
covering the surfaces we have made.
Above us on the overpass, tar and gravel
car-scattered, but here blackberries swell
in speckled light, hard green knots of cells
among white shreds of flower, and still vines travel,

leafing and leaning into sun, as we
lean into their shadow. Three years back we rode
this passage in the dark, an edge in us
crowded with possible fruit, stippled with day.
We cycled through that margin, into a field
of lengthening afternoons, a surety

to last us years together and years apart
from Carolina. Now, held fast in our
habitual sun, we tilt south, needing more—
the shifting light of woods-edge to remind us
of first uncertainty that, tended, turns
into a constant chaos we can inhabit,

make a home in. Let's walk as the wild
grape moves, with curving purpose, toward shade
and back to the shine of noon, breathing in
the saving scent of honeysuckle, jewelweed,
summer grasses and our sun-warmed hair,
dizzying our senses, pulling us toward
each other's verdant bodies, summoning
a salve, a word to keep us: we live here.

"I'm Going Back to North Carolina" first appeared in the 2012 Nazim
Hikmet Poetry Festival anthology.

Hand Me Down My Walking Cane

Anna Lena Phillips

"Hand me down my walking cane"
Ralph Blizard and the New Southern Ramblers

Pull the back door shut and drop the latch.
Hand me down my walking cane. I won't look back.

Rosin up the bow for one more tune.
How can I play this refrain and not look back?

You catch a glimpse or two; he steals them away—
keep hold of what you can, and don't look back.

I've done it all my life—kept misery
at bay with one firm line: Don't look back.

Anybody asks you where I've gone
say I've left on the midnight train and won't look back.

Look neither back nor forward—that's the way
to love. Drink up your wine, and don't look back.

Is that you, standing just beyond the porch light?
Well, step in out of the rain, and don't look back.

"Hand Me Down My Walking Cane" first appeared in the 2012 Nazim
Hikmet Poetry Festival anthology.

Inter-mix'd
Lynne Thompson

Although he chose to lie with another
and turned absent father because of it,

Daddy decided to hitch his fate to Mom.
Mommie was fair in complexion (one clue

being her name—cobbled together from Low
German, middle Dutch, some old English:

hesel, hasil, hasell, hazel) but even that
hegemony didn't deter him, proud as he was

of his Igbo; proud he faced windward after
the Bight of Biafra/Bight of Bonny; pleased

to feed his family cassava & taro root. In a time
when many thought he would not have been,

he was learnéd. When he looked at her, when
she spoke her name, he might have thought

*Let the Angler fit himself with a Hazle of one piece
or two set conveniently together* (Cox, 1677)

or the note of hasel springeth (Hazlitt, 1864).
He might have thought of her as his *hazel-wand* or

hazel-hooped or a dervish of *hazel-wizard* healing his
scarifications, her body fully salt-fish and chickpea.

What he thought is lost to time but never can be.
He anointed himself with oil of hazel: see his

children sitting, as Virgil said, *beneath the grateful
shade which hazles, inter-mix'd with elms, have made?*

To Blackness

Lynne Thompson

As it happens, I have never tired of blackness—its Marcus Garvey,
Raisin in the Sun, Tuskeegee airman. Its Strivers Row and liver lips;

its Dred Scott, Freedman's Bureau, Scott Joplin. Some say black is
swarthy, gloomy, evil, fiendish, but we all spring from the tribes—

Ashanti, Bobo, Fulani, Wolof—their cowrie shells and krobo beads
sewn into our fading fabric. I don't know much about my native
blackness;

my daddy, he say *Igbo*, the only word he can give me, but it's the only
word
I need to get the old folks to remembering that in Igbo *ututu* is
morning,

abali is night, and in any mirror, my *ihu*—my face—is always black.

How I Learned Where We Come From
Lynne Thompson

When she wants him for the late meal, she calls
supper soon Kingstown-man, curried goat, sticky-wicket

and he responds, testy, *not yet ready, Bequia-woman,*
Anglican church, basket with no handles.

We children, we laugh, head for the hills
and the tall sweet-grasses, listen for the lilt

of frangipani tantie. She call *come in now*
pigeon peas, mangoes, poor man's orchids—

then we run, for true, and supper is all
cassava root, callaloo, very little sugarcane

and we're in it all at once: choirsong above
Mt. Pleasant, Port Elizabeth, harp of Paget Farm

till Father, he say *no*, defends his slipped-on wishes
for Soufrière, Sans Souci, Wallilabou Bay

and so on into the evening, calypso and steel drums,
a little Rasta and Bob Marley for us young'uns

until, finally, we are no longer black ironwood—
wood that will not float.

There Is a Zabava
Nicole Yurcaba

There is a zabava,
and everyone is singing
the songs about the birds;
there is a pearl inside me
that wishes I could play
Dedushka's mandolin which rests
in its battered leather case
because I feel, at times,
that all we as Ukrainians have
is each other and the music:
the squalling trumpets,
the plucked banduras,
the daring dentsivkas,
Diduk's silenced mandolin
and the tribal drums
that move our feet
and sway our hips
and preserve on our lips
that intricate language,
those spider-web secrets
that are preciously ours.
I spread my arms
and I embrace the notes,
I intertwine with the rhythm;
I am in flight like sokoly
who flies close to Sura's face
and kisses the clouds;
I am flying home
to Ukrayina's green fields,
those wheat-washed fields
from which my family
should never have been separated,
those fields to which I try to desperately return,
and I fail and instead of sokoly,
I am the phoenix crashing
in flames to a world
in which I cannot land;

all that cushions me
is the music,
the music which resides in my hollow bones,
the music which crept through my grandfather's bones
and my father's bones,
and drove them to dance.

I Hear My Ancestors Singing

Nicole Yurcaba

"So shall your descendants and your name remain"--Isaiah 66:22
My bloodline banished me to this occupation.
After all, in the sacred tongue, "Yurchak" means "farmer".

Like my ancestors,
I scythe the waving wheat;
I reap the golden rye;
I plow, row by row,
I sow the seeds in winter and spring
in the open fields.

The sun kisses my face;
the labor tones my muscles;
the dirt stains my skin;
the scythe's wooden handle blisters my palms.

As I scythe the waving wheat
and I reap the golden rye
and I plow, row by row,
and I sow the seeds in winter and spring
in the open fields,
like my ancestors

I sing the folk songs of stronger generations before me
in the sacred tongue;
I lift my minor voice
to the white-pocked sky
and to God
and to the embracing breeze;

in those moments
I am my great-grandfather
who toiled behind horse and plow,
who blistered his hand scything for the master,
who nicked his fingers mending saddles,
who bellowed the ancient songs
in the mother tongue.

Papa, Tse Kholodno (Papa, It's Cold)

Nicole Yurcaba

I.
He raised us to never fear the cold,
to stifle shivers when the wind and the wars
cut our skin, reddened our faces:
"Don't complain," he'd say,
"It would be minus-thirty in Kyiv today."

My gloved hand would find a home in his bare one,
and I would eye the cracked, dry, pink-white skin
of my father's hands while we marched
through snow-laden woods.

With each of the wind's bites, the shivers would rise,
and I would hunker my face further into my coat's
fur-lined hood.

Finally, I would peek my face from its warm burrow
as I tugged at his hand and I would mutter
"Papa, tse kholodno!"—"Papa, it's cold!"
"Skoro bude vesna"—"Soon it will be Spring,"
was all I was told.

II.
A sledgehammer's lengthy swing,
the toppling SMASH!—Lenin's statue
falls, his face meets the street.

The midnight sky burns orange
as set afire tires bleed black into night.

Our faces blaze with rage, with heat,
with exhaustion, with blood
and with a gloved hand
I press the cellphone to my frostbitten ear.

"Hello?" he says from 6,000 miles too far away.
"Papa! Tse kholodno!" I scream as another flame
spews from the pyre, "Lenin has fallen!"

He laughs a hardy laugh,
a Cossack's laugh, deep and wide
like the Dnipro,
and then he declares
"Todi, dochka, na sohodnishny den' tse vesna"
—"Then, daughter, today it is Spring."

Lost in Translation
Nicole Yurcaba

I.
Somewhere in venturing from the Cyrillic
to the transliteration and then into the English
loss, entropy, decay occurs; emotion vanishes;
true intent disappears. The natural meaning
sloughs.

All that remains is Anglicized blankness.

II.
Baba wrapped
our tiny fingers in her wrinkled hands
as she prayed in the language we were forbidden
to speak and to write outside her home;
when she finished she sent us away with a squeeze
of the hand, a kiss on our smooth cheeks,
and a loudly uttered "Z Bozom! With God!"
We crossed ourselves after releasing her hand,
quietly repeated "Z Bozom!" before leaving her presence.

III.
The return to the mother tongue is the sweetest nectar:
traveling from the Anglicized blankness,
transitioning to the rough-edged transliteration,
morphing into the orthography of our blood land—
challenging adversity
by celebrating undeniable roots. We,
like the language, become incomprehensible to those
who do not recognize their historical suffering.

IV.
Too many years, yes, it has been
since Slavic words rolled
from our tongues. The melting pot
has voided, hulled, made null,
our beings, our articulations;
and our combined memories
cannot recall the intricacies

of Baba's foreign prayer.
We have become Gogol:
trapped, clawing, dying.

V.
Pen in hand,
the tip to the paper's white,
the reconnection occurs
via the physical act of spilling
ink in coordinated chaos,
in script as chaotic as history.

(How appropriate!)

Names—written,
sentences—concreted, inerasable,
constructed subject-verb-object.

The energy travels
via fingertips and arms,
through the neck
to the mouth,
where nerve-wires trip the tongue,
strike up the vocal chords
and summons the Old East Slavic beast
that provokes palatized vowels.

With each pen stroke,
the blankness is combatted,
adversity conquered,
identity reclaimed.

Identity. Reclaimed.
Voice regained.

Addiction

R.G. Evans

It was a miracle—
like Shadrach, Meshach and Abednego—
the way my father passed
his hand through a candle's flame
and never once got burned.
A little black wisp of smoke
and he'd smile at me and say
Do it fast and the flame'll never hurt you.
Never was much of a listener,
all I heard was *Do it and hurt.*
And Daddy, what do you do
when you can't tell your fingers from the flame?

Originally published in *Tiferet.*

Husk
Justin Walmsley

how could we know
— could I write of suffering?

the sweat of the beer can fleeing downward,
causes the coaster to stick to the bottom
and I sigh, upset

this *cannot* be suffering
yet, I sigh and i am defeated to know
like a child staring at the husk of some other dead insect
held up by brown grass and beige
that change has occurred

we too suffer change
we two are privileged

Composition #1

Lynne Thompson

If I say the woman who birthed me betrayed me,
you may think that woman *badly distilled, needful*;

but if I say she who betrayed me was herself betrayed,
you may think of the woman as *gesture, exile, spilled out*

because when we think of exile or the innocent gesture
—if there's any such thing as a gesture that's innocent—

we should also think *intolerable mirror*, the mirror never
reflecting that it could become obsession or that it might,

perhaps, just peel away. And if I say *peel* or *blunder* or *mercy*,
you might think my vision too fragile and you're half right:

from somewhere, unbidden, a woman waylaid by my birth,
whistles: *here's a swaying bridge, cross over, compose the dark.*

*The italicized phrase in the final line appears in the Larry Levis poem,
"Elegy With A Chimneysweep Falling Inside It."

An Open Letter from Alexander the Great to his Father
Amoja Sumler

Dear father
I remember you standing the height of a disapproving God,
me lost in your shadow.

I was taught when you were half my age you stood memorable as
mythology,
strong as the Minotaur
Master of men on the battlefield.
I have seen you proficient with sword and spear.

I have seen you victorious leader,
hunter questing.
Your name, dripping honey, banded about on the tongues of young slave
girls.
"Philip the conqueror!" they cried.

They cried.

How that must have pleased you.

Each of your successes punctuated with the requisite sacrifice
of blood
and semen.

I have seen you
vicious and vain
shrunken as a boil freshly popped
reduced to morning lies to my never reassured mother
doing her best to hold on to greatness and sanity.

Irony the laughing mistress you could not bend.
All the others supplicant, submissive,
I have seen you pissing drunk,
Achilles tendon exposed
a mammoth of manliness.

I have seen me:
eyes bulging, wide mouthed covered,
a mere fraction of you
and cheaply jealous.

Once younger,
I was caught trying to climb Mount Olympus,
because they told me that's where the Gods were.
I saw you father, did you see me?
Ascending
three points of contact
moving hand over fist
free of fear wanting nothing
for the first time ever
leaving you
to want for my balls.

I am writing from Persia.
Laying on fabrics from further east still,
soft as Arachne's own work.
I was never a rough man you see.
They call it silk.
They say it reminds them of
my armies' phalanx movements.

One hundred Centurions,
one man tight into the next
seamless into one body (like lovers)
with a thousand protruding points of death.

Were you ever stabbed father?
Did they hurt you father.
Do you hurt father?
Father.
I hurt.
Half a world, broken beneath my will.

Father, do you see me?
Do you see me climbing mountains?
Am I a man yet father?
Father. Am I enough yet?

Am I Man enough father?
Father. Love me?
Do you love me?
Have I killed and fucked,
and broken enough?
Am I broken?

Father.
Do you break?
Are you broken? Father.
Can I stop? Can I stop yet?
Is it enough?
Can I be your little Alexander?

If I climb high enough, will you watch?
Father , I can.
I assure you I can.
I will climb until you say, "my child, I am proud!"
Crush, until you smile and blow a kiss to your diligent boy;
Your loving son.

I am just waiting
on permission from you
to stop
breaking.

Photosynthesis *(for my son)*
Teresa Mei Chuc

for my son –

How can I convince you
that you do have chlorophyll,
that you can take the sun's
energy and turn it into sugar?
Produce something sweet inside of you.
Take the waste people breathe out
and make it into something that
will keep you alive, that will keep
those around you alive, create oxygen.

Why do you say that this metaphor
doesn't work, that you don't have
the powers of a plant, that nature
didn't intend you that way?

Look, how you twist and turn
towards the light.

"Photosynthesis" was first published in *EarthSpeak Magazine.*

Wondering Why While Wandering Where

Andrew Manyika

Time spent walking the earth wears down the sole

Dust
Whilst packing the last of our prized possessions,
Moving things we thought we'd planted,
And letting emptiness reprise it's position,
We turn our home into a mere house
and I come across an old pair of shoes
They are well-worn and from the process of so becoming,
 are worn down. Scuffed at the front, warm to the feel,
And torn at the heel
I try to remember them being new,
And all the places they've been since then
It amuses me to think that shoes, having tongues but no eyes,
cannot tell of all the places they've seen
So, these shoes, that have moved me through every plausible place,
I now remove to put them away
In so doing, I catch sight of the heel and it's curvature strikes me,
I am wondering where the rubber that had been this sole has gone
In leaving it's imprint on the earth,
Did it also leave little pieces of itself behind,
Like calling cards for the ground?
And all that displaced dust?
Did it creep into the grooves of the sole so that,
Knowingly or not, I brought little pieces of everywhere,
Here, to our home.
Which, once these shoes are packed, will become only a house?
In them I've walked so many miles, so many miles…

Time spent walking the earth wears down the soul

Home
We've packed everything that needed packing,
And stacked every box that needed stacking,
And as strangers gut my home,
I say as little as possible because every sound now carries an echo
And every echo makes it harder to let go and realise,

This is no longer my place,
As silence takes hold of every audible space
I stand looking at the thin film of dust on all the surfaces,
You grab my arm and we remark together how it settled so easily on our dreams
Like little pieces of everywhere stifling little pieces of us
Dreams die slow deaths and there is nothing gentle about their passing,
All it takes for a pen to bleed is, in the right place,
A touch and a little pressure,
As tears blur my vision, I think perhaps my soul is much like a pen
You grab my arm again and tell me,
"It's time"
You are not wrong,
We have filled the quota of memories to be made here
And it's a long way to the new house,
Between here and there are so many miles, so many miles….

Floating in the Ocean

Greg Miraglia

I feel like a piece of
wood floating in the Ocean.
I drift, and drift endlessly,
people only grab me
when they're broken,
lonely, or desperate.
Each time I'm sent
back out to drift,
each time I'm the only
one with strength,
each time I wish somebody
strong could grab me,
somebody that doesn't need
to be saved.
There's lots of water --
out here.

I feel like a piece of
scrap floating in the Ocean.
Water pulls me, pulls endlessly,
survivors use me,
survivors, victims,
or the lost ones.
Each time their tears
fool me into staying,
each time their hugs
fool me, *maybe they'll stay?*
Each time their reliance
makes me question my strength.
They'll toss me back out,
seems to be the way
of the Ocean.
There's lots of water --
for floating.

A Sort of Self (a soliloquy)

Patsy Asuncion

It's quiet here   wherever I am
a kind of quiet I've never met
with breathing room   between thoughts

to sort myself   to look back on myself
a different angle   in the mirror of myself.

I wish I'd been safely parented   before I
parented. Bad habits never died they just
got passed on   to the next gen.

I mourn not having a   maternal moon
to guide my efforts with my children.

Long after they found   their own ways
I did learn to forgive myself   when I
accepted that I was a   mosaic mother.

Perfectionist   critic   five-star general
mixed with   nurturer   protector   muse.

It took me more than fifty years to
find my own true love   a giving guy
who accepted   every part of me.

I think now it took me decades   to have
myself   so I could have him.

I know the best of my life was the
last of my life   when I filtered crystal
clear importance   from dark chatter of the day.

My centerpiece of living large was unlocking
the door to   creativity   at every stage of age.

Picasso said *it takes one   a long time*
to become young, to see with fresh eyes
to play on new paths   to breathe life into dreams.
My only regret is that I didn't learn sooner
to choose beginnings   not accept endings.

Jalopy
Patsy Asuncion

She was stolen   shiny new   outside
a tenement for a joy ride   then abandoned
in a back alley   No anti-theft devices
in those days   just next of kin   to fender
troublemakers   When they found her
they thought she was lucky   just
a busted headlight   bloody dents
and pigeon-toed tires   probably
the reason thieves   dumped her

Once healed   she proved   a good car
who kept good traction   whenever
she drove her stepmother   home
from the neighborhood   tap   Mechanics
saw her potential   caught her interest
with books   Interior lights   a tough
engine   ensured   high performance
in school despite   being   left
alone a lot   on the street

Tomboy antics in the alleys   scarred
all four tires but she put up   a poker-face
Two crashes   shorting her electrical
started migraines   every time she used
her turn signals   Surgery on ball joints
and quality oil seemed to quiet   cranky
squeaks   when she rolled   She paid
attention   keeping her trim   in top shape
to slow depreciation   unlike some friends

Maintenance doesn't stop   life's odometer
    Rust spots   on her once flawless finish
increased   each winter   Young cracks
in her underbody   began puckering her
mainframe   Cheap gas had been   no
problem but then started   upsetting her gut
Chronic allergies insisted   more air filter

changes   Not surprised   each time she
was traded   She   didn't choose   her owners

Sold now as   vintage   she is   adept
a classic from the day   the only one
to make it   out of the old neighborhood
While memory settings   have lost old
details   she recalls   important choices
    running even in bad weather   starting
    while missing parts   finding her way
    regardless of   confusing road signs
    optimizing   her standard   components

Everything and Nothing

Patsy Asuncion

It was the best of times, it was the worst of times, it was the age of wisdom,
it was the age of foolishness... it was the season of Light,
it was the season of Darkness.

A Tale of Two Cities, Charles Dickens

High school graduation
our singular event in 1964, our season
to make a difference.

Believing
new heavyweight champ Ali – we could
float like a butterfly, sting like a bee, we could
rise from poverty like the Beatles, we could
enjoy equal opportunity in the Promise Land of new laws.

That was the banner year.
Johnson's Civil Rights Act
thickened conviction –
    power to the people was possible.
Poitier's Oscar
Martin Luther King's Nobel Peace Prize
Frazier's Gold
– all in '64
confronted conventions.
Fresh-faced, virtuous Medicare
helped the sick and elderly.
Even big tobacco took a hit
from the Surgeon General.
    I have a dream pulsed our senses.

Yet, it was the first year of Viet Nam,
a twenty-year war
coupled with twenty years of domestic violence –
King's assassination
Riots
Kent State and Jonestown – knuckling
us into bruised disbelief of the Establishment.

The '90s saw the demise of Russia and the Cold War,
but homegrown rampage
raged on – Columbine, Oklahoma City, Waco.

These past fifty years, our parents' work ethic
anchored us.
We made a difference
through our labor, which defined our identity.
Retirement is merely redirection.

That same 1964 *I can*
attitude carries over to this new century
of live stream, Blu-ray, nooks, smartphones, face transplants,
in-vitro kidneys, stem cell livers, even asteroid Pluto. We are
the *high-def* seniors of the world, engaged
and running
like the Everready Bunny.

Between the Making and the Ruining
(for Michael Rewa)
R.G. Evans

Someone once told me about sonnets,
how they're connected to the breath:
an Italian like the steady rise and fall—
inhale, exhale—of Sophia Loren's bosom,
and the less subtle English like blowing up a balloon
to burst it at the end. But here near the middle of this
American sonnet, where is our breath? Caught
inside our throats, too tight to come or go,
like arteries or freeways not built for so much volume,
or infinite, all prairies and salt flats, one
eternal emptying of the lungs—everywhere . . . everywhere?
This is what happens, see. You start with this
and end up with that. This isn't about you or me
or the weird alchemy of words that can bind us.
Is it?
And here it is so late and too long already,
and I haven't even mentioned love, how things like it
come apart so easily.

Originally published in *Lips*.

The Last Poem
Tiffany Austin

I.

I glance at your nakedness,

some cracks here and there, in the tub;
we had to make sure you wouldn't fall again

and you finally looked after the water,
no more driving yourself to the hospital,

me to another town, on the porch for some
wind—air too small.

After you visited your brothers and sisters to say goodbye,
they still didn't understand, yelling softly to the ones who were left,

who waited for body's disappearance, who saw last love,
"Why didn't you tell us? Why didn't you let us come?"

We tried to explain through not looking that you wanted it this way.

You didn't want the runny eyes. I knew that the morning I made
too much breakfast for you. I finally got the eggs right, so the softness
sank,

the rice, remembering you standing at the stove, showing me once,
twice.
I loved to see you cook early in the morning or late at night.

I would laugh at you.

II.

He didn't mind that laughter.

When you brought the tray up to him he simply said,
this is too much.

But you were trying to feed him more seconds, more breath.
You finally understood walking up the stairs.

Then you only arrived with coffee, half an egg spread out so it looked
like a full meal.
This feeding is tricky.

III.

I was trying to feed him more breath.

One of those nights when the sky was too loosed, we watched *Bitter Rice*
in Italian.
They in bed, me at the bottom, sitting on the floor, my back against the
bed post.

There was a scene with a man touching a woman, and I thought if
anyone walked in
they would be embarrassed—

mother, father wrapped as some ginger attempting to sit cross-legged
and
a daughter watching love making.

Rosebreasted. I see my great grandmother gently waking you and my
mother with a kiss.
You are startled because, there, in an upstairs bedroom is the twice
feeling of water.

I was made in this.

Later, I wanted to say rice as you rubbed your stubble in the mirror that
last lucid day,
But it came out as laughter; not at you,

I was laughing at this hesitancy,

one flies, and then another, not at the same time, but safe in this too
loosed sky.
You are ascending the stairs, not falling this time,

you were to me as a birdsong.

Aegean Sea
John Most

water waters a body of water in the distance
umbrella slanted a vision imperfect descends
blocking the moment dishonest light ribbons only
for movement sensing does the formation of
memory formations form this beach nowhere
back and forth keeping track of tracking the lines
little then a room kinetic in a room hotel in a room
unvexed undecidedly wishing wishes to be
retracted peeling flecks clear a view dear onto view
window onto view giant transports all into a
slipping slippery sense of things transient like liking
skips of shells broken losing the lines little in mind
sand addressing others' matters gated by motions
rippled returning having decided only to find
finding a memory's map to be a mistake recovered
pinning down a fear separating possible scenarios
from a single occurrence by entering the chaos
another light lights nothing stumbling into the
incorrect group the returning water returns
procedures out now restored are not the same
tracking the keeping track of tracking the lines little

"Aegean Sea" was previously published in *Newport Life Magazine.*

The Last Canary Speaks

Sara Robinson

We live between moments
It's between those moments
a space of time
between blinks where we
crowd in our tears   laughs
great books   not-so-great poems
nuts and bolts into pressure cookers

It's the moment between
solar cyclones, between
trips to the store,
where trapped in aisles
we pause   read end notes
of protein bars and dried plums

It's the moment between
the finish line and thirteen
steps before we hear something—
a sharp sound   a cry on the fourteenth one
while someone begs for Ben Gay in
bomb-smothered air

this moment   this vast space
creates another space with
no defined depth or width
but with great height over which
we cannot see moments ahead
or behind and we cannot tell
if there are ash marks on our shoes

But we find this one
immeasurable moment, next to
a curb in a black backpack
where inside time yawns
like a big cat after swallowing
the next-to-last canary whose moment

stopped suddenly.

the decade the rainforest died*
Teresa Mei Chuc

the deer did not
stop running
leopards
climbed into trees
that could not
hide them

the douc langur
and the white
cheeked gibbon
cursed at the
metal gods
we flew

raining
on them
as they burned
from napalm

elephants
choked on the
smoke of gunpowder
and poison
their steps
a strange
rhythm
as they tried
to fly

the thunder
of bombs echoed the steps
of elephants

tigers exploded
as they stepped
onto landmines

in a forest covered
with leaves

dead from
Agent Orange,
fallen trees and
decomposing
bodies of animals
and people

the earthworms
were washed away
in monsoons
with soil that could
no longer grab onto
roots

the Javan
rhinoceros
and the wild
water buffalos
that were still
alive
wandered
aimlessly

weary
with M16s
and AK-47s, we
marched quietly
and steadily
not knowing
why we were
killing each other

*For ten years, the U.S. Air Force flew nearly 20,000 herbicide spray missions in order to destroy the forest cover as well as agriculture lands in key areas of southern Viet Nam.

"the decade the rainforest died" was first published in *Kyoto Journal*.

Shepherded Sheep
Neal Hall

We are shepherded sheep
day dreaming in fallow fields of dreams

in fallow fields of " build It " and

the fools of faith will come to kneel before it

It - this one thing called by two names
this double dealing back to back

double face of evil
halo'ed and horn'ed
adorned in black and white whose intersecting edges bleed gray
to make sure the fools of faith lose their way

It - this one thing called by two names
this father and son, double dealing us
separating us into secular and non-secular

double dipping us, pitting us against us to kill us one by one
till thy kingdom be done

Double dealing deities and devils

dealing heavens and hells that do not exist
myths and tales that tells us to bend the knee
before devils and deities double dealing

in selling heavens and hells that do not exist

We are shepherded sheep

layered in layers of doomsday lies and lies of everlasting life beyond this
life by anointed, appointed listeners hearing the call of their calling

to call us to bow the head and bend the knee

to offer up offerings to an economy of trinity

selling heavens and hells
selling freedom from fears by playing to our fears

It - is but this one thing,

this trinity called by two names
this double faced jewel of

biblical piracy, of biblical proportions
pilfering, pulling the wool over the foolish eyes of sheep
to fleece and rob them of their wool

We are shepherded sheep,

day dreaming in fallow fields of dreams
in fallow fields of " build It " and

the fools of faith will come to kneel before it

Veneer
Neal Hall

Artificial perfection,
evenly spread superficially across surface irregularities,
concealing surfaced inner imperfections;
outward manifestations of inner fears of fear, and
choreographed lies we dance around
to spin around the truth

An ill-fitted counterfeit
hundred dollar bill, stretched
to fit over a folded wad of ones

a forged friendly smiles
laminated the surface of our hate

a smooth silky satin sock
we weave to cover rough feet
we dance around the truth upon

Veneer:

This laminate,
this conceived hell-resistant immaculate conception
we fabricate to wear, to cover our trail to cover our tails
to cover when we steal,
when we kill,
when we bear false witness in the dark
abyss beneath the surface of those
loosely adherent layered laminates:
thou shalt not steal,
thou shalt not kill,
thou shalt not bear false witness

Veneer

marquise masquerading masks of cleansing and rebirth,
facades that are no more than,
a more pleasing appearance,
no more than a more desirable surface material
of skim coat surface lies, thinly coating

150

who we really are lurking beneath the lies
of soul cleansing and rebirth

Veneer

this Inlay of two, overlying one, added on top
to divide the one into two halves one
was never meant to be: a you, a me,
a wrong, a right, a black, a white,
synthesized black light emitting
florescent composites of manufactured darkness,
casting unenlightened shadows
we hide our surface woes beneath

Veneer'd

We are, manufactured mannequins,
still life surface paragons, dressed up
in monogramed window dressings,
facades beneath which we bleed sanguineous denials,
shrouded in diaphanous layers of artificial truths
we cover our true selves in to appear
more loving in our false love,
more tolerant in our synthetic tolerance
more human in our inhuman inhumanity
we falsely appear to be,
to cover over what we have become . . .

an ill-fitted counterfeit
hundred dollar bill, stretched
to fit over a folded wad of ones

a forged friendly smiles
laminated the surface of our hate

a smooth silky satin sock
we weave to cover rough feet
we dance around the truth upon . . .

where will you stand when it rises
Joanna Lee

the sound of jackhammers
ceased, cranes stand
expectant. they tell me
there is growth here,
but the streets are broken
open, slip
sores to the ebbing
flow of days.

still, they pull fewer bodies
from these waters
than one might think;
a tribute to the sinking power
of upward mobility.

in the Bottom,
men work the corners
in teams. you hardly see
the flower-seller
anymore.

the night runs through
fog-off-the-river shadow,
streetlight over slick
cobblestone. like so many things,
headlight distances
can be deceiving.

the first train mourns slow
through middle trestle
headed West; the second
runs canalside at speed,
coal in darkness.
their rhythm blurs time and distance,
and suddenly we could be anywhere,
and in it lie forgiveness.

there is a single petal in red
at the center of the pipeline,
a dead finch on brick sidewalk
come morning. the jackhammer
is awake.

on the near side of the hill,
the bottom floor of Sanger Hall
is seeping[1], and they are pulling
bodies into the elevators.
upward mobility.

i never used those shafts
if i could help it.
eight flights then was the easy part[2].
we find our history like headlights:
not so bitter now, not so dead.

there is growth here, too.

[1] "VCU's Sanger Hall remains closed after water main break,"
R.Daudani. www.nbc12.com. Nov 26, 2013. What no headline or article
mentions: VCU Medical Center's morgue resides in the bottom floor of
Sanger; immediate effects of this fact, real or imagined, are my own.

[2] The gross anatomy (cadaver) lab was on the eighth floor.

"where will you stand when it rises" was initially published in *Richmond
Arts Review* (2014).

Straddling the Line
Greg Miraglia

We want order, but we are unordered,
like stars and celestial bodies in
space.
We set up nature trails to stay with nature,
to remind us we are human, to remind us we
are animals, to remind us we are mammals
of the highest order,
order,

but we chop away the trees, and pave over
their roots, we put up signs, we put up fences,
we put up rules.

Do we see our hypocrisy?
Do we see ourselves?

We want to be tribal and sporting to believe
we are still hunters, to believe we are still predators,
so we gather our gear, and hunt deer or turkey
or bear,

but we fence in acres, we transport animals,
we use automatic weapons, we pollute hunting with
bullets and bullying, instead of the ever-ending chase
or wait, we use helicopters and ATVs.

Do we see our actions?
Do we see ourselves?

We go outdoors to be among the fields and trees
at night with a bonfire lighting and warming us,
as fire did to our ancestors,

but we bring trucks, we bring cords and generators,
we bring gadgets, and the circle of natural light
in transformed into a massive of bright unnatural
light and noise.

Do we see our effect?
Do we see ourselves?

If you want nature, have nature, but
accept that it is unsafe sometimes
        cold sometimes
        mosquitoed sometimes
Don't make it civil, because once the wilderness
we long for is paved, fenced, signed, and ruled,
it is unsatisfyingly the end of our natural connection.
Don't leave the trees
Don't leave the river
Don't leave the fish
Don't leave the rabbits
The deer
The grass
The leaves
The hills
Don't leave them–
To politics
To humans
To *civilization*

The Sky
Greg Miraglia

Where did my light go?
Once it brightened every living
thing,
once my stars would deliver
a beautiful blue night.

Humankind has ended that,
always inside hooked to
their machines,
and sometimes their technology
takes them for a solitary walk.

At night my stars cannot compete
with the lamps, and lights from
each town.
I once illuminated the darkness,
now it illuminates itself.

Tiny Fires
Aimee Suzara

Listen.
We   *butiki* slid bulbous bellies
                over smooth rocks   ,   we

gentle butanding
turned the sea into milk.

Now   Nestle carton bobs
on the fetid waters of the Pasig.
      Open sewers gape   like torn bellies.
Children hunt
for metal parts and plastic sacks.   *Pandacan*
birthed poets, but now it sits
in the shadow of the fuel tank   *ripe for disaster.*
                             (Unassailable evidence)
Obtuse CEOS gaze down metallic towers
cursing shanty dwellers   clicking mahjong/kicking sipa/
butchering pigs
in the hell below.

We   bloodstain *tutubi*
wings thirty-feet spanned,
could be seen drifting between storms and songs.
We   30,000 eyes   began
with gills
in shallow edges
of the river.   Could   breathe underwater.

I tell you this because the thing is happening and you may look upon
your cracked sheaths and see a thing that we were not. You may call
yourself John/Susan/Kate wear Old Navy smile when someone thinks
you look like Brad/Jennifer/Angelina. You may tip cowboy hats, sling
guns on hips, shift the gears of German sports cars. But one day the
game is up:

The ones who gave you compliments regard your eyes
detect your bloodstain wings pressing through your skin.

This is why it is important
that you listen
and remember   we were not
jars of talcum powder.
                    Not Master Creams and syringed serums cramming
drugstore aisles.
              Not teenaged strippers in red-light districts with faraway
looks,
waiting for the 'Kano to take us home.

Not the Aeta woman begging
at the edge of the landfill
where tiny methane fires light up the mountains
of what the world has tossed away.

We   *butiki*
We   *butanding*
We   *tutubi*

Could breathe underwater.

Acknowledgments

Indranil Acharya, translator of Susil Mandal's work, is Associate Professor in the Department of English at Vidyasagar University in Midnapore (West Bengal). He obtained his Ph.D. on Yeats and Eliot in 2004. He also completed one UGC Research Project on Contemporary Australian Aboriginal Fiction in 2008. Dr Acharya had been the Deputy Coordinator of the UGC Special Assistance Programme on the documentation and translation of the oral and folk literature of the dalit and tribal communities in West Bengal. He is also implementing one UGC Major Research Project as the Principal Investigator on the documentation, translation and analysis of Bengali Folk Drama in the context of endangerment. His first published book is *Beyond the Sense of Belonging: Race, Class and Gender in the Poetry of Yeats and Eliot*. He has also edited a book, *Survival and Other Stories: Anthology of Bangla Dalit Stories*, with Orient Blackswan. Another edited volume entitled *Towards Social Change: Essays on Dalit Literature* (Orient Blackswan) has been published in 2013.

Sara Allam was born in Egypt in 1989; she received her degree in Mass Communication and Journalism from Cairo University. She has two published collections of poems: *Without a trace for a kiss* (Elain Publishing House, 2013) and *Untangled the buttons of loneliness* (Elain Publishing House, 2013).

Patsy Asuncion found public education her ticket from inner-city Chicago, which led to professional writing during her public school career. Her poetry and short stories are in *Prevention Magazine* and numerous anthologies (recently in Chatter House Press' *Reckless Writing*, SUNY's *Healing Muse*, L.A. Loyola's *The Truth About the Fact*, NFPS' *Encore*) and online journals – UK's *Female First* and Laughing Fire Press' *Today & Yesterday*. 2015 publications include her first poetry collection, Laughing Fire Press' *Cut on the Bias*, and works in two anthologies from Artemis Journal and Unbound Content. A bi-racial grandmother of five, she promotes diversity through arts, including hosting an open mic for all artists.

Tiffany Austin grew up in Missouri and presently lives in South Florida, where she teaches. She received her B.A. in English from Spelman College, her M.F.A. in creative writing from Chicago State University, her J.D. from Northeastern University School of Law, and her Ph.D. in English from Saint Louis University. Tiffany Austin has published poetry in *Callaloo, Obsidian III, Coloring Book: An Anthology of Poetry and Fiction by Multicultural Writers,* and *Warpland.* Her poetry chapbook *Étude* was recently published by Finishing Line Press. She has attended the *Callaloo* Creative Writing Workshop at Texas A&M University and a summer workshop at the Fine Arts Work Center in Provincetown, MA, and has received a residency fellowship at the Virginia Center for Creative Arts, and the Gwendolyn Brooks Poetry Award in Chicago, IL.

Heather Banks was born in Nebraska, published her first poem soon after moving to Massachusetts at age 11. She double majored in English and art at Oberlin College, where several poems were in the literary magazine, *Burnt Star.* She taught English at Tunghai University in Taiwan for 2 years, then at the high school and college levels, including at the University of Maryland, Montgomery College, and Howard University. During half of her 40 years in the DC area, she morphed into a writer/editor at the Smithsonian, NIH, a scientific society, and several nonprofits and contractors. Heather has read at numerous venues in Maryland, Pennsylvania, and DC. A featured Regional Poet at the 1999 South Central Modern Language Association, she has published in literary magazines, such as *Dryad* and *Sun & Moon,* and two DC anthologies (*The Poet Upstairs* and *City Celebration*). Her chapbooks, *Still Life Without Pomegranate* (2008) and *Split Rail Fence* (2014), were published by Eyrie Heath Press. After "retiring" and moving to Harrisonburg, VA, in 2011, she is busier than ever.

Michael Bassett holds an MFA from Vermont College and a Ph.D. from the University of Southern Mississippi. He is the author of four poetry collections: *Karma Puppets* (2003), *Waiting for Love to Make My Phone Explode* (2007), *A Train Dreams of When It Was a Killer Whale* (2009), and *Hatchery of Tongues* (2014). His poems have appeared in hundreds of journals and dozens of anthologies. He is the winner of the 2005 Fugue poetry contest judged by Tony Hoagland and of the Joan Johnson award. He lives in Bluffton, SC.

Lady Caress is a National Performance Poet who uses a mix of beat boxing, music, and storytelling to capture audiences of all ages. She has dedicated her life to the art of communication as both a poet and public speaker. As a National Poetry Champion in 2010 at Pi Kappa Delta, Lady Caress has continued to impact audiences outside of the performance

160

realm. She has designed and executed public speaking and poetry workshops for Upward Bound, YMCA and S.T.A.R.S., an organization designed to bring extra-curricular activities to at-risk youth. She served as Spoken Word Poetry Consultant for Iowa's National Night Out and coached both high school and collegiate students in competitive Poetry and Prose performance pieces. While her work often extends to off stage ventures, she still captures audiences with her unique set of poetic nuances. She has featured at The Marshall Arts Room, Love Jonz Spoken Jazz Set, and Sunday Spoken in Dallas, TX. She has graced the stage at Bus Boys and Poets in Washington, DC, Say What Poetry in Des Moines, Iowa, and took home 1st place twice at the Jacksonville, FL Amateur Night. She has performed on BET at the 365 Black Awards and Season 4 of Verses and Flow on TvOne.

Angela M. Carter was raised in a Virginia farming town. She moved to England, for nearly five years, after receiving a one-month scholarship to study at the University of Bath. She returned to Virginia with a new-found confidence, and voice. Her first full-length collection, *Memory Chose a Woman's Body* (unbound CONTENT, 2014), is a poetic journey, and memoir, that spotlights the effects of the silences endured after abuse, neglect and depression. Angela is a 2014 Pushcart Prize nominee, nominee for the 2015 Virginia Library Literacy Award (poetry), a motivational speaker, arts advocate, a painter and photographer. She has been published in *Deep Water Literary Journal, Whurk, Vox Poetica, Premiere Generation Ink, City Lit Rag, The Word Ocean, Worst Week Ever, Our Stories Untold, Gutsy Living,* and several anthology publications. She is an advocate of the healing ability of the arts. Angela M. Carter lives in Harrisonburg, VA.

Teresa Mei Chuc is the author of two poetry books, *Red Thread* (Fithian Press, 2012) and *Keeper of the Winds* (FootHills Publishing, 2014). She was born in Saigon, Vietnam, and immigrated to the United States under political asylum with her mother and brother shortly after the Vietnam War while her father remained in a Vietcong "reeducation" camp for nine years. Her poetry appears in journals such as *EarthSpeak Magazine, The Good Men Project, Hawai'i Pacific Review, Hypothetical Review, Kyoto Journal, The Prose-Poem Project, The National Poetry Review, Rattle, Verse Daily* and in anthologies such as *New Poets of the American West* (Many Voices Press, 2010), *With Our Eyes Wide Open: Poems of the New American Century* (West End Press, 2014), and *Mo' Joe* (Beatlick Press, 2014). Teresa's poetry is forthcoming in the anthology, *Inheriting the*

War: Poetry and Prose by Descendants of Vietnam Veterans and Refugees. Her poetry book, *Song of Bones*, is forthcoming from Many Voices Press in 2016.

Nicelle Davis is a California poet, collaborator, and performance artist who walks the desert with her son, J.J., in search of owl pellets and rattlesnake skins. Her most recent collection, *In the Circus of You* is available from Rose Metal Press. She is the author of two other books of poetry: *Becoming Judas*, available from Red Hen Press, and *Circe*, available from Lowbrow Press. Another book of poems, *The Walled Wife*, is forthcoming from Red Hen Press in 2017. She is editor-at-large of *The Los Angeles Review*.

Daniel Dissinger, Queens, NY-based poet, is the co-founder and COO of Poetry Teachers NYC. He founded an online Audio Zine, In Stereo Press (instereopress.com), in 2008. Daniel currently teaches at SUNY College at Old Westbury, and is completing his doctoral work at St. John's University, where he is also an adjunct in the English department. Daniel's first chapbook *tracing the shape ...* was published in 2012 by Shadow Mountain Press. He's recently been included in the next Great Weather for Media anthology.

R.G. Evans' first collection of poems, *Overtipping the Ferryman*, won the 2014 Aldrich Press Poetry Prize. His poems, reviews and fiction have appeared in *Rattle, The Literary Review, Paterson Literary Review, Tenebres* (translated into French), and *Weird Tales* among other publications. Evans was a featured reader at the 2014 Dodge Poetry Festival, and his original music, including the song "The Crows of Paterson," was featured in the 2012 documentary *All That Lies Between Us*. Evans teaches high school and college English and Creative Writing in southern New Jersey. Find out more about him and his work at his website: www.rgevanswriter.com

Stanley Galloway is the founder and organizer of the Bridgewater International Poetry Festival. He has taught at Bridgewater College for 20+ years. His first full-length poetry collection, *Just Married* (unbound CONTENT, 2013), deals with the adjustments of a new bridegroom. He is the author of *The Teenage Tarzan: A Litarary Analysis of Edgar Rice Burroughs' Jungle Tales of Tarzan* (McFarland, 2010).

Jesse Glass lives in Japan with his family. *Man's Wows*, Glass's erasure poems from 1982, were recently featured in a study of 20th century conceptual poetry titled *Wiederaufgelegt; Zur Appropriation von Texten und Buchern in Buchern*, edited by Anette Gilbert from the German scholarly press Lettre [Transcript] Verlag.

Joshua Gray returned to the Washington DC metropolitan area in 2014 after spending two years in India. His most recent book is *Steel Cut Oats* (2015, Red Dashboard Press), a collection of poems about food and its traditions. "Puja" was nominated for a Pushcart Prize.

Neal Hall is a medical-surgical eye physician and graduate of Cornell and Harvard Universities. An internationally acclaimed poet, he has performed poetry readings throughout the United States as well as Kenya, Indonesia, France, Jamaica, Morocco, Canada, Nepal, Italy and India. He is the author of two award-winning books of poetry: *Nigger For Life* and *Winter's A' Coming Still*, which have received numerous awards. His third book, *Where Do I Sit*, will be published in summer of 2015.

Aimee Herman is a Brooklyn-based poet and performance artist looking to disembowel the architecture of gender and what it means to queer the body. Find Aimee's poems in *Troubling the Line: Trans and Genderqueer Poetry and Poetics* (Nightboat Books), in the full-length collection *to go without blinking* (BlazeVOX books), the chapbook *rooted* (Dancing Girl Press), and in the full-length book of poems *meant to wake up feeling* (great weather for MEDIA). Aimee is an adjunct professor at Bronx Community College.

A. Logan Hill grew up just north of Harrisonburg, VA, in an old house by a small town off the highway and is currently a poetry candidate in the MFA Program for Poets & Writers at the University of Massachusetts-Amherst. His next publications will be a novel & a chapbook, *This something*, a collection of appropriations from texts on Nothing.

Sirwan Kajjo, born in 1986 in Syria, is a journalist and poet based in Washington, DC. He is the author of two poetry books in Kurdish. He moved to the US in 2008 after being granted asylum. Prior to moving to America, he lived in Lebanon for two years, where he worked as a reporter. He writes in Arabic, Kurdish and English.

Beth Konkoski is a writer and high school English teacher living in Northern Virginia with her husband and two children. Her poetry has been published in numerous literary journals including: *The Potomac*

Review, Gargoyle and *The Aurorean*. Her chapbook, *Noticing the Splash* was published by BoneWorld Press in 2010. She has work forthcoming in *Saranac Review, The Clementine Poetry Journal*, and *Gyroscope Review*.

Dawn Leas' poems and book reviews have appeared in print and online journals such as *Literary Mama, San Pedro River Review, Interstice, Southern Women's Review*, and *Poets' Quarterly*. Her chapbook, *I Know When to Keep Quiet* (Finishing Line Press, 2010), is available in print and Kindle versions, and a collection of her poems appears in the anthology, *Everyday Escape Poems* (SwanDive Publishing, 2014). In past lives she was a copywriter, freelancer, an admissions director and middle-school English teacher. Currently, she is the associate director of the Wilkes University M.A./M.F.A. Creative Writing programs and resides in northeastern Pennsylvania. She's a contributing editor at *Poets' Quarterly* and *TheThe Poetry*.

Joanna Lee, poet and professional muse, has never formally studied writing, though she earned her MD from the Medical College of Virginia in 2007 and a further MS in Applied Science from the College of William and Mary in 2010. Her poetry has been published in a number of online and print journals, including *Caduceus, Floodwall, scissors and spackle* and *The Dead Mule School of Southern Literature*. Her second full-length book of poetry, *the river and the dead*, is forthcoming in 2015 from unboundCONTENT. Under the big bright umbrella of "River City Poets," Joanna coordinates poetry readings & events from Shockoe Slip to South of the James in Richmond, VA.

Andrew Manyika is a Harare-based writer, poet, & comedian. In the ten years in which he lived in South Africa he rose to prominence within the local Spoken word industry; he was the winner of the University of Johannesburg's International Students Poetry Competition in 2010, Gauteng Province champion in the 2011 Drama For Life Poetry Slam, and placed second at the National Grand Slam. He has performed at the WordNSound International Festival, been selected to Macufe Festival, and was a producer of the inaugural SLAM For Your Life, which is now an annual production at the National Arts Festival in Grahamstown. Andrew has written commissioned poetry, and performed at, among other events, TEDxJohannesburg (2012), Izimbongi Poetry Festival (2012) and The Harare International Festival of the Arts (HIFA) 2014. He has shared stages with the leading poets & comedians from both Africa and abroad.

Greg Miraglia's poetry has been published in *Symmetry Pebbles, Aerogram,* and *The Garbanzo Literary Journal.* Some of his poems have also made it into *Unbridled,* an anthology from Red Dashboard LLC. Greg's plays, *Jump* and *Getting Down* have been produced in the 2011 and 2013 Second Stage Short Play Festivals by the Auburn Players. For the last two years he has read work beside other poets in the Fall and Spring Poetry Readings held by the Schweinfurth Art Center in Auburn, NY. Greg writes movie reviews. He is a member of the WriteOn Writers group of Cayuga County and is a former member of the James City Poets of Virginia.

Susil Mandal was born in April, 1959 in Palpur village of Gosaba Police Station in Sunderbans. He was initiated to the world of poetry in the school established by an Englishman, Hamilton in the Sunderbans. He became a faculty member in the department of English at Narendrapur Ramakrishna Mission Ashram in 1982. Susil Mandal developed an intimate bond with mainstream Bengali Poetry, beginning in the 1980s. This Dalit poet has contributed poems to leading Bengali literary magazines like *Desh, Udbodhan, Matrishakti, Baisakhi* etc. He has appeared for many poetry reading sessions on radio and television channels. He has attended many national and international conferences on poetry. His most noteworthy volumes of poetry are *Ak Akash Geetabitan, Anuchar Taranga, HeemSandhyar Batas, Nirjanatar Baibhabe,* and *Ananta Aswiner Shishire* — all published by Dey's Publishing, in Kolkata. His *Selected Poems* was also published by Dey's Publishing in 2015. He has also received two major awards — Loksakha Sammanana and Banani Puraskar.

John Most lives in Crozet, Virginia. He is the author of *Field, Persephone,* and *Atelier.*

Sarah Elizabeth Murphy is a writer/poet/artist who splits her time between the Appalachian Mountains of Virginia and the New England coast in Connecticut.

Michelle O'Hearn, "MiCKi," is a native Virginia poet/singer/songwriter and producer actively working the performance circles of Central Virginia, namely Fredericksburg, Orange, Culpeper and Charlottesville. "SoulMate" was first published in one of Michelle's early chapbooks and became the lyrics to her song by the same name that was published in her 2nd music collection, *Peace & Quiet* (2014). Her latest works include a 3rd music CD, *Bye Greener Pastures* (2015) and the CAT Bus Lines winning poem, "The HARP Temptation" (2015), that can be seen in the UVA Special Collections Library and was read as part of the Virginia Festival of the Book in Charlottesville.

Anna Lena Phillips' recent projects include *A Pocket Book of Forms*, a letterpress-printed guide to poetic forms, and *Forces of Attention*, objects designed to help people interact with screened devices. She teaches at UNC Wilmington, where she is editor of *Ecotone* and Lookout Books; she is also a contributing editor for *American Scientist* magazine.

Joani Reese has had fiction, creative nonfiction, and poetry published by more than 70 print and online journals. Reese won the 15th Glass Woman Prize for her prose poem, "Simulacra," the first Patricia McFarland Memorial Prize for her flash fiction "The Cost," and the Graduate School Creative Writing Award from The University of Memphis for her poetry. Reese has been poetry editor for *THIS Magazine*, senior poetry editor for *Connotation Press*, and is currently general editor for *MadHat Lit*, the online presence of MadHat Publishing. Reese has two published chapbooks, *Final Notes* and *Dead Letters*. Her first full collection of poems and stories, *Night Chorus*, was published in 2015 by Lit Fest Press.

Sara Robinson, a native Virginian, retired from a career of technical marketing and publications to pursue creative writing. Her inaugural work, *Love Always, Hobby and Jessie* (2009) was a memoir devoted to the stories of her parents and their tumultuous marriage which lasted more than fifty years. Sara has appeared twice on *Artist First Radio Network* as well as on the *Hilda Ward Show*, and *Artistic Expressions*. She is poetry columnist for *Southern Writers' Magazine*, poetry editor for *The Virginia Literary Journal*, and founder of the Lonesome Mountain Pros(e)Writers Workshop. Her poetry has been published in several journals and anthologies. Her poetry books, *Two Little Girls in a Wading Pool* and *Stones for Words* (Cedar Creek Publishing, 2012 and 2015, respectively) have been nominated for Library of Virginia Literary Awards. In 2014 her workshop published its first anthology, *We Grew Wings and Flew*. She teaches a course on contemporary poetry for UVA/OLLI and has conducted poetry workshops across Virginia. She currently resides near Charlottesville, VA.

Albert Russo has published worldwide more than 85 books of poetry, fiction and photography, in both English and French, his two mother tongues (Italian being his 'paternal' tongue; he also speaks Spanish and German and still has notions of Swahili). He is the recipient of many awards, such as The New York Poetry Forum and Amelia (CA) Awards, The American Society of Writers Fiction Award, The British Diversity Short Story Award, The AZsacra International Poetry Award (Taj Mahal Review), the Books & Authors Award, several Writer's Digest poetry and fiction Awards, Aquillrelle Awards, the Prix Colette and the Prix de la Liberté, among others. His work has been translated into a dozen languages in 25 countries, on five continents. He has garnered several prizes for his photography books, Indie Excellence Awards, The London Book Festival awards, The Gallery Photografica awards (silver medal), among others. Some of his photos have been exhibited at the prestigious Museum of Photography in Lausanne, Switzerland. The Mayor of the Big Apple, Michael Bloomberg, has lauded his two photobooks on Paris and New York. Albert Russo was also a member of the 1996 jury for the Neustadt International Prize for Literature which often leads to the Nobel Prize of Literature. Latest Prize: Best 2013 Unicef Short Story award in defense of childhood worldwide, entitled: "Revenge by proxy / Vengeance par procuration." He lives in Paris.

John Saleh is a Kurdish poet living in Washington, D.C. He writes in Arabic and then translates into English.

Jeff Schwaner lives in Staunton, Virginia. His work has been featured recently in the *New Orleans Review,* and his most recent projects include the broadside *Drop Everything* and the haiku coaster set *Night Walk on Cape Cod*, both printed at St. Brigid Press. Work from his newest books *The Drift* and *Moonlight & Shadow: Mei Yao-ch'en, An Imaginary Portrait* can be previewed on his blog *Translations from the English.*

Amoja Sumler is a poet and social activist known for fusing the art of the intellectual into the familiar. As "The Mo-Man," he tours nationally and headlines spoken word festivals like Write NOLA in New Orleans and Rock the Republic in Texas. He has also presented at social advocacy conferences like Long Beach Indie Film Pedagogy Conference and the world renowned Furious Flower as a panelist representing The Watering Hole writing collective. Home base is Arkansas.

Aimee Suzara is an Oakland-based Filipino-American poet, playwright, and performer and educator whose mission is to create poetic and theatrical work about race, gender, and the body to provoke dialogue and social change. Her debut poetry book, *SOUVENIR* (WordTech Editions, 2014) was lauded as "a powerful meditation on history and the legacies of race, family and identity" (David Mura), and her poems appear in numerous collections, including *Phat'itude* and *Kartika Review*. Her performance work has been supported by YBCAway Award, National Endowment for the Arts, East Bay Community Foundation commission; selected for the One Minute Play Festival, Playground, APAture, and Utah Arts Festival; and staged at the Berkeley Repertory Theater, CounterPULSE, and others. She is a Spirited Woman Award Fellow and two-time resident at Hedgebrook Residency, and an alumna of VONA (Voices of Her Nations Arts Foundation) program and Mills College, where she received her M.F.A. in 2006.

William Sypher worked as an English professor for 26 years in five Middle Eastern countries: Iran, Saudi Arabia, Bahrain, Qatar, and Oman. Living in the desert under a frequently featureless sky inspired him to try to populate that canvas with images, but he paints only with words. In Oman he wrote essays accompanying landscape photographs in the book Oman, My Beautiful Country. A native of West Virginia, William has resided with his wife and best critic in Charlottesville, VA, since 2010.

Haley Tennant is a student at Bridgewater College. Her work has appeared in the college's newspaper, *Veritas*, on several occasions. She is an English major.

Lynne Thompson is the author of two chapbooks, *We Arrive by Accumulation* and *Through A Window*, as well as the full-length collections *Start With A Small Guitar* and *Beg No Pardon*, winner of the Perugia Press Book Award and the Great Lakes Colleges Association's New Writers Award. Recent work has appeared in *Prairie Schooner, Weave, African American Review, Fourteen Hills*, and *Crab Orchard Review*, among others.

Michael Trocchia is the author of *Unfounded* (FutureCycle Press, 2015) and *The Fatherlands* (Monkey Puzzle Press, 2014). His work has appeared in journals such as *Asheville Poetry Review, Baltimore Review, Camera Obscura, Colorado Review, Mid-American Review*, and *Worcester Review*. He writes and works in Virginia's Shenandoah Valley.

Justin George Walmsley lives in Toronto where he works as a barista in both an Italian bakery and an independent coffee shop. A few years ago, he graduated with a double major in Film Theory and Creative Writing out of York University and is currently enrolled to begin his Masters in Creative Writing at the University of British Columbia. DADA and Surrealism heavily influence his avant-garde style of writing, which is suggestive of latent themes such as self-reflexivity and the absurd. He is currently working on a collection of poems, titled *Uterus Stories*, as well as a prose piece titled *moral CITY*.

Nicole Yurcaba, second place winner of Australia's Poetry Sans Frontieres Hemingway Contest, is a Ukrainian-American writer and internationally recognized poet. Her love and dedication to words has propelled her into the arms of such publications as *The Atlanta Review, The Bluestone Review, Midway, The Tishman Review, Southern Women's Review, Vox Poetica*, and many others. Yurcaba's first poetry and photography collection *Backwoods and Back Words* is available through Unbound Content on Amazon, and her second collection *Ukrainian Daze* is forthcoming. She is an English professor in West Virginia.

Selected Titles Published by Unbound Content

* 9 7 8 1 9 3 6 3 7 3 5 7 4 *